Tales for the

OUTHOUSE

A COLLECTION OF FUNNY SHORT STORIES

ROD URQUHART

STONE'S THROW PUBLICATIONS

Layout: James Dewar
www.stonesthrowps.ca
Front Page illustration by Susie Kockerscheidt

Library and Archives Canada Cataloguing in Publication

Urquhart, Rod, 1954-, author
     Tales for the outhouse : a collection of funny short stories / Rod Urquhart.

ISBN 978-1-987813-05-0 (paperback)

     I. Title.

PS8641.R687T34 2015   C817'.6   C2015-901645-2

Printed and bound in Canada

Also by the Author, Talk Turkey with Urqey

1 2 3 4 5 6 7 8 9 10

~ Dedication ~

To my ever-loving younger sister, Tracy, a double breast cancer survivor, who brings such joy to so many people, and she is not even aware of it. Her presence on this earth makes it a warmer place. And despite all I did to her when I was younger, she turned out just fine!

~ Foreword ~

Enough talk about me. Let's talk about you. What do you think of me?

As my wife says all the time, "It's not always about you."

But, in this book, I get to indulge myself in many past memories, mostly with myself as the main character. These are non-fiction humour stories, true to life, as best as I can remember.

I also included some of my columns printed in The Era of late and also some early stories I did for The Era-Banner on the Loch Simcoe Monster – stories that generated a lot of interest. I heard from some parents that their children wouldn't go in the water for fear of the Monster after they were published.

This is my second book – the first was Talk Turkey With Urqey – and was another true-to-life non-fiction humour book. It generated quite a lot of response.

I want to thank John Slykhuis for editing this second book, and offering his insightful comments. I also thank Rose Thompson for looking over the manuscript and finding some troubling typos. I'd also like to thank Bruce Annan for editing my first book. Bruce now has a second career as a book editor and is quite busy! Thanks also to my dear friend Susie Kockerscheidt (now that's a mouthful, eh?) for her cover illustration.

Like the first book, you'll see the response to a chapter I have written by my sister Tracy Campbell. Sometimes I think she's funnier than I.

She has two chapters in this new book. Also responding to a chapter is Big John Sibbald. Big John also gets the final word in Chapter 39. Again, sometimes I don't feel too funny with such exceptional writing. But sometimes, Bob's your uncle!

I write like Ernest Hemingway – short and concise. No, no, don't take that as an inference that I'm another Ernest Hemingway … far from it. That's why this isn't a very big book, but it's packed full of short, humourous stories. I sincerely hope you enjoy my second effort!

Hopefully, you still have an outhouse!

Rod Urquhart

(I can always be reached at – roderick.urquhart@gmail.com)

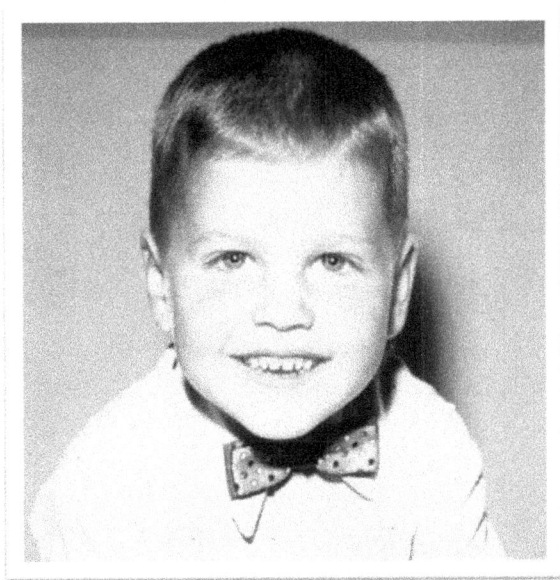

The author at age 2.
Submitted photo

~ Table of Contents ~

~1~ Too much ketchup, I guess

I have this older friend. I should say he's a young 84. Let's call him Bwana, although he's quite the proper English gentleman.

About once a week he'd call me up to go out for a nice meal. Well, this one day was different – he wanted to go to McDonald's. He felt like a Big Mac. Quite frankly, I don't usually eat at McDonald's, but every once in a while I get a craving for a Big Mac. So he picks me up and off we go to the local McDonald's.

We both get the Big Mac Meal – Big Mac, fries and a drink. We sit at a table near a window and for some reason this McDonald's is quite packed with burger eaters.

We start to eat and remember we are both very hard of hearing. I should get a hearing aid, but I'm too vain. He probably should too.

Bwana says to me with a mouth full of Big Mac and fries, "My friend got a monkey."

I said, "Your friend got a monkey. Why would he get a monkey?"

Bwana repeats only a bit louder, "My friend got a monkey, I said."

So I repeated, "Why in blazes would your friend get a monkey?"

So an agitated Bwana, screams out in this McDonald's,

"MY FRIEND SHOT HIMSELF MONDAY!"

Well, everyone in this packed McDonald's turns and looks at us, even the cashiers and take-out workers. They all looked a bit stunned by Bwana's revelation.

Taken aback at the news, and remember Bwana is age 84 and thinks a lot about the end of life, I then said to an obviously agitated friend, "Well, he should have gotten a monkey."

Bwana didn't think this was too funny, but then he smiled at our folly in miscommunication. And, we talked a bit about his friend and why he shot himself.

Now whenever I see Bwana, if someone he knows has passed away, I just say, "He (or she) should have gotten a monkey," and we both get into a better mood.

See, without a hearing aid, you can get into all kinds of trouble!

POSTSCRIPT – Bwana is still doing fine and will probably live to age 100.
He always says he looks 60 and has the women fighting over him.

~2~ And they wonder why I don't come!

FOREWORD – Raymond's (Tracy) response to this chapter follows, as in my first book.

Whatever possessed my dear old dad to drive to Florida, with three kids and a wife, towing a large sleeping and cooking trailer, with an old six-cylinder Ford Fairlane 500? All that damn way to Florida with three kids ranging in age from six to 14 in 1968.

My God, I have many friends who now have a luxurious Ponderosa in Florida that invite me down. I don't fly. "Why don't you drive?" they say. After you read this, you'll realize why a road trip to Florida is out of the question. I'd rather walk from Nepal to the Base Camp of Mount Everest than travel by vehicle to Florida.

Now my sister Tracy, age 6 at the time, who I call Raymond, has threatened me not to include this chapter in this book. She said she won't read it and won't pass it out to her friends. But, being a writer with integrity, I carry on with the challenge.

My other sister, Adrienne, who we simply call Big Ad, was age 10 or 11 and a real rascal.

All I remember about that long, long trip to Florida, what with their low speed limits and a six-cylinder car towing this massive camper, was it was a long, long trip. I remember looking out from the back seat constantly and just seeing miles and miles of highway, overpasses and lots and lots of traffic. Ohh, I still get the shudders today just thinking back.

What made matters worse, was we were little kids – we couldn't crap on demand. And my Dad being the mad demon that he was, would only stop for gas or overnight to rest. So at these gas stops we'd all head to the bathroom. To this day, I can't crap on demand, so needless to say, us three kids in the back were all severely constipated. Our only venue was to let out 'gas'. Well, we gassed ourselves silly in the back of that 1966 Ford Fairlane 500. It was just a 'farting festival' all the way down to Florida.

And old Russell the Rascal didn't really have a game plan. We never stayed in motels or hotels. He would find some place to park and we'd sleep in a large camper trailer, usually cooking our meals in there too. I remember one night he just pulled into a closed gas station for the night and parked. Across the road was a greasy spoon/tavern and that's where we all had dinner. Let me tell you, my Dad had guts, because it was a rough, drinking crowd in there.

Guess where we spent Christmas? (I forgot to mention off the top, but my Dad was a school principal and we were headed to Florida on Christmas break). Well, unbeknownst to me, the reason for this trip to Florida was to meet another family he knew at a Florida trailer park.

Christmas Eve we arrive at the trailer park in Fort Lauderdale or as Aase calls it, Fort Liquordale and the park is full!! We drive all the way to Florida, towing this massive trailer, mile after mile on the road, only to find this park full!

So my Dad, being the ever-resourceful man he was, just pulls over near a bridge, off the highway to the park, and we camp in the trailer for the night. That was Christmas Eve. The only good thing about that is, it was warm and we were very near to water.

Of course we are kids, and its Christmas Eve, so we had no trouble getting to sleep to see what Santa would bring us in the morning. (Yes, I knew there was no Santa at age 14, but I knew I'd be getting presents, or at least I hoped so).

We wake up in this trailer camper and there's presents stuffed in the tiny corners for us three kids. Raymond was the most excited cause she was a true Santa believer. Tracy went on and on about how could Santa find us so far from home and stuck on the side of a highway? That was until Big Ad informed her "There is no Santa. It was Mom and Dad, you idiot." A kid's childhood hero shot down in a single sentence. It devastated Raymond for a long time.

We ventured outside and we were very close to the ocean. The tide must have come up in the night, because we children walked the beach and found a baby octopus trapped in a small water hole. That amazed us – the first octopus we had seen up close.

Well, back into the Ford Fairlane 500 and off to the trailer park early Christmas morning and we got in. We spend two weeks there – no swimming pool, no place to swim, no amenities except a large Community Centre with showers and a meeting room – one of the most boring times of my life. More on this later if I have room!!

POSTSCRIPT – Big John, Bob, Raymond and Phyllis, maybe now you'll understand why I don't want to take the drive to Florida.

Raymond phoned this morning from Florida and said she made it down in two days.

I don't know how long we were in that Ford Fairlane 500, but it seemed an eternity.

Raymond's (Tracy) response is the next chapter as I said off the top.

~3~ Spoiler Alert!

By Tracy Campbell
In response to the previous chapter.

My memory of this famous trip varies from Rod's but I was that much younger so some things are a little fuzzy. I do know that Rod is still only six years older than I am and if it was 1968 then I would have been 8 years old at the time. It was a different era and we didn't have any handheld electronics to keep us occupied for that long, smelly car ride (I don't think we had seat belts then either!).

I actually don't remember stopping overnight and thought we drove straight through. My father wouldn't let my mom do any of the driving so she played word games with us kids or slept most of the way doing the 'snap and drool'. Unfortunately, at one red light when he was behind the wheel, my dad fell asleep too. Thankfully the car beside us beeped their horn to wake him up and we continued safely to our destination.

Being the youngest, I had to sit on the 'hump' in the middle backseat squished between my older siblings. The reason that I didn't want Rod to tell this tale is because I was the one with all the gas in the back seat! After reading chapter 16 you'll discover this may have been the best 'arse'nal I had for getting back at Roddy and Ad.

When we finally arrived in Florida on Christmas Eve, we couldn't get into the trailer park as it was first-come, first-served and the campground was full. The plan then was to get up early the next morning on Christmas day and get in line for a camping spot. So we drove around looking for a place to stay for the night and remarked how we all felt like Mary and Joseph. Finally we found a fish and tackle store on the beach that was still open and they let us stay overnight in their parking lot. Not ideal but better than a stable!

Finally out of the car and in Florida, with a lovely warm evening, we kids ran in the sand kicking in the waves, laughing and playing on the beach in the pitch dark. It was to our absolute shock the next morning when we found a baby octopus far from the tide resting in a small pool made in the sand. It was an amazing sight and we were thankful that none of us had stepped on the little pink baby the night before. (Too bad we didn't have Smart Phones then to snap some photos.)

But the real surprise that strange Christmas morning was to find the Barbie and Ken dolls that I so desperately wanted under my bunk in the trailer! I could not believe my eyes. How did Santa find me...in a different country, not in my own bed but a pull down cot, in a trailer that didn't even have a fireplace chimney, in a parking lot where we didn't know we would be staying the night, so far from home? It was a Christmas miracle.

We were up early because it was Christmas morning wanting to open our gifts and we had to quickly pack up to get in line for the trailer park. We managed to get into the park, get settled and then we met up with our family friends the Warden's and their three very cute young sons. Could this holiday get any better? I carelessly played in the foam and the surf all week long and then it was time to head back home but I didn't mind because now I had my new dolls to play with! I still couldn't get over my amazement that Santa found me.

I just couldn't stop talking about how this wonderfully incredulous event occurred in my life. After listening to me go on and on and on, I think my poor sister lasted over 1,000 miles (we hadn't been introduced to the metric system yet), before she'd had enough. Finally Ad said to me, "There is no such thing as Santa, STUPID! Mom and Dad bought those dolls, brought them with us all the way from home and put them under your bed! You are such an idiot."

I didn't see it coming at all. I really had NO idea.

Although I was eight-years-old at the time, it was a more innocent era (no cable or internet) and I didn't have so much as an inkling that Santa did not exist...seriously. I'd asked my mother in the past how Santa could be at the G.E.M. store and at the Richmond Heights Plaza (Hillcrest Mall hadn't been built yet) at the same time and she explained to me, "Santa can't be everywhere so he has helpers that pretend to be him." Made perfect sense to me, being a wide-eyed naive child.

I can remember it like yesterday because my world changed that day. I don't think I said another word for the rest of the trip as I had a lot of information to process. That is how I learned there is no such thing as Santa.

~4~ The Outhouse Affair

Back many, many years ago, when I was about age 10, I was a Boy Scout. Now, following one Boy Scout meeting at the local church basement, it was announced a group of us would be going to Oxbow Trail Boy Scout Camp.

I can't recall exactly where that camp is, but I know it's up north and nowhere near a lake. I decided to ask if my good buddy, Dougie Nicholls could come along as well. The officials said it was okay as long as he paid his way, like me, for this week-long adventure, even though he wasn't a Boy Scout.

We were all driven to the camp and told to bring sleeping bags and our necessities; food and lodging would be provided. We were also told to bring good flashlights. And it would be hot, the middle of summer.

We arrive at the camp. It has a large cabin with three-high bunk beds attached to the wall all around the perimeter. It could sleep pretty well all 30 of us – with the exception of Dougie Nicholls. Because he wasn't a Boy Scout, he got the dregs – no bunk bed and had to sleep on the wooden floor in his sleeping bag.

Following dinner, a campfire, we retired to bed using just our flashlights for light. Well, after we settle in, there's a male scream from the floor – it's Dougie Nicholls – someone had placed a live garter snake in his sleeping bag, which he didn't discover until he got in it for the night.

It scared the living crap out of him.

No camp counselors came in, so we just let the snake out of the cabin door and we went to bed. That was night one.

After a day of craft-making and lunch and dinner, then another fire, we retired to bed once again. Once again we changed by flashlight into our pyjamas and settled down for the night. Again, there's a scream from the floor and it's Dougie Nicholls – some little fiend has chewed a big wad of bubble gum and placed it inside his sleeping bag. We tried to pick this gum out of the sleeping bag, but it was a miserable job and we were all tired. We did the best we could and then left Dougie to his own devices. That was night two.

We never found out who did these things to Dougie. We never found out why, either. At our age, it took quite the creative mind to come up with these dastardly deeds to do to Dougie.

Night three, I'm sound asleep and all the sudden there a lot of yelling and screaming by the biggest kid in the group. Apparently Peewee, as we called this rather small boy, had gone to the outhouse down the lane in the middle of the night and somehow dropped the big guy's good flashlight down the hole.

There was a lot of yelling and screaming and sobbing. Apparently the big kid decided he's going to lift Peewee by the ankles down the hole to retrieve his flashlight. Peewee was sobbing, but the big kid had his mind made up – and off down the laneway they left on the way to the outhouse.

They came back about 10 minutes later, Peewee no longer smelled like a rose, but they had the flashlight.

That's about the only memorable things that happened at Boy Scout Camp. I left them shortly after and started taking boxing lessons, which were much more enjoyable. I still don't want to think about 'what if the big kid's grip slipped?'

POSTSCRIPT – A true story.

~5~ Frying for Fish

Many, many years ago, when I was a young lad of 18, I had quite the adventure with my good friend – we'll call him Misener.

We were at his cottage on Lake Bernard in Sundridge when we both had a brilliant idea – let's go into the bush and fish to our heart's content!

Misener's dad, Ken, and his uncle, Jim, had a hunting camp way back in the bush – I mean way back. Misener and I had to go shopping and outfit ourselves with complete neck and head gear to protect ourselves from mosquitoes, gloves to protect our hands, wear long pants and long-sleeved shirts. This despite the fact it was a solid 90 degrees Fahrenheit outside.

Misener's dad Ken drove us way into the outskirts of Sundridge. I can't even remember just where he took us. But we ended up on a dirt road with an old, old farmhouse at the end. On the porch of this farm house, way into the bush, were three boys sitting on rocking chairs. Deliverance with Burt Reynolds had just come out and I wondered what we had gotten ourselves into. All one of the boys needed was a banjo. It was a little unnerving.

His dad just stopped the car, said goodbye and off Misener and I trekked down some overgrown pathway into dense bush. We had our backpacks on, complete with enough food for four days, our sleeping bags, our fishing gear and tackle and enough beer for about one day. They didn't sell cans much back then so carrying bottles of beer was daunting.

So there we were, walking in the bush, loaded down with about 50 pounds on our back in backpacks, in 90 degree weather, sun shining, completely covered up for the hordes of mosquitoes. His dad said it was about a four-hour walk in to the camp.

So Misener and I trek along these trails. After about two hours, we come to a fork in the pathway. And get this, there's now road signs, explaining which road leads where – and this is two hours into dense bush. And we see one of those old Argos under a tarp down one road – one of those six or eight-wheel contraptions for travelling in the bush.

So Misener says this way and we head off down one of the roads. About an hour later, we come to another four-way meeting of the trails and again they have road signs. Again Misener says this way and off we go down this road. Another hour and we reach our destination.

Well, we come upon a clearing and sure enough there's a rather large cabin, a hunting camp, complete with a large propane cylinder out the back. It's full of propane – how they did that is beyond me – and it keeps the fridge cold, runs the stove and two overhead lights. So after our four hour walk in the extreme heat, we can't wait to get our beer in the fridge.

Inside there's a series of bunk beds, a large eating table, the fridge, stove, counter and not much else. But a lot of Playboy pin-ups on the walls. There is a rather stinky outhouse for doing your business. But having a fridge that works was pure heaven. In a short time we both enjoyed a beer thanks to a good working freezer in the fridge. (Misener and I enjoyed our beer back then).

Once we had unpacked, keep in mind we never took off our hooded mosquito hats with netting that tied under your shirt to protect your neck, we headed off to see the fishing lake.

It was a lake about 150 yards by 100 yards – not very big, but apparently full of lake trout. There was an old rowboat on the shore. We looked down at the water, it was not the kind of water one could swim in. We saw platoons of leeches swimming around. I'd never seen this kind before. They had orange diamonds down their back and all were about 9 inches long – quite large for a leech. We reasoned, I guess that's why the fishing is so good. And it was.

We retired to the cabin – how it was constructed so far back in the bush is way beyond my comprehension. The lake wasn't big enough to get a plane in and snowmobiles were just starting to come onto the scene. The trail wasn't big enough for any kind of vehicle, except maybe an Argo. Still mystifies me today, and as Ken and Jim have passed away, I'll guess I'll never know.

Well, Misener and I make a good lunch after our long walk, enjoy another of the scarce beers and head off to the rowboat. Now all fishermen have tall tales of fishing, but this fishing was phenomenal. The fish did everything but jump in the boat. We caught our limit in about an hour. It seemed that you just drop the line in the water and wham! You'd have a good-sized lake trout. We couldn't fish that long in one outing, because the rowboat would take on all kinds of water. It was only safe for about one hour.

We headed back to the cabin - about a five minute walk with our fish - and prepared a magnificent dinner, and tried to drink beer with full mosquito netting on our heads.

At night when we settled down in our bunk beds, complete with our mosquito netting on because the inside of the cabin was filled with those nasty creatures, making it very hard to sleep as they whirled around both our heads. When all was quiet, then we heard all the mice in the ceiling. There was a real party going on in the ceiling with all the mice. Then we heard them. They were invading our space for any food crumbs. On went the lights. I had a small throwing knife and I tried to pin one against the wall. Funny thing was their hole to get into the living space of the cabin was behind a Playboy pin-up. I demolished that pin-up throwing my knife at it to get one of these damn mice!!!

The mosquitoes and mice were driving us nuts. We barely slept. After about three days of fishing all day and hardly sleeping at night, it was time for the long trek back to Deliverance land and our pick-up by Misener's dad – a pre-arranged time. We had long ago run out of beer. Only, now we had to carry out a whack of lake trout that we had caught.

We walked out and met Ken and he drove us to the cottage. We both couldn't wait to have a shower and get cleaned up and actually use a flush toilet again. We managed to bring out enough lake trout for Misener's parents and us to enjoy a huge, fresh fish fry dinner. And, it was simply delicious. Misener's dad and mom were thrilled with the dinner.

POSTSCRIPT – It wasn't too many years later that Ken died – way too early.

Ken had taught me my long-time love of the Argos football club and he was also a diehard Leafs fan. I enjoyed the Leafs as well until they treated Darryl Sittler so shabbily – then I stopped in honour of my memory of Ken. Sittler was his favourite player.

I'll never forget Ken coming up to his cottage in Sundridge on a Friday night after a long week at work and cooking up a mess of chicken livers. I've never tried them to this day and I still remember the smell of Ken cooking up his favourite dish.

~6~ Out into the wilds of Sundridge

After the last chapter, you can imagine, I spent a lot of time in Sundridge. One of my favourite places on earth – but that was back in the 1970s, so I imagine much has changed. We were just 'wild and crazy guys', doing whatever the hell we felt like and usually getting away with it.

Misener's mother Phid was most accommodating for most of our shenanigans. For some strange reason, we were definitely into fishing. Not really hunting, but definitely fishing.

One day Misener's cousin, The Proud One, who also rented a place up in Sundridge, said he knew of this great fishing lake, where the fish actually jump in the boat. It was way, way back in the bush at the cottage of some former famous owner of the Argos that the only way to get there was to fly in. Apparently, way back in the bush was some mansion that the owner and visitors regularly took float planes into. And this mansion, which was on a huge lake in the bush, had this smaller lake that had a boat on shore.

The Proud One said the only way in was some old logging trail. Being stupid and young, The Proud One figured I could drive my 1974 Toyota SR5 on this old logging trail and we'd have the time of our lives catching all kinds of fish.

The Proud One, where he now lives in Victoria
in this undated photo.
-submitted photo

To this day, I don't know how I did it. The consequences would have been horrendous if my car broke down or even got stuck. The Proud One and myself drove on this old logging trail for a solid hour to reach this famous fishing lake.

The branches were constantly scraping my car, the path was completely overgrown with stumps and fallen branches. Being young and foolish, I just carried on, driving over everything in my way, thinking I was in some sort of tank. Yes, we made it to the fishing lake, and yes there was an aluminum boat on shore with oars for rowing.

We parked my car and grabbed our fishing gear. It was hot, about 85 degrees Fahrenheit. Well, we fished all day, tried every lure in our tackle boxes and didn't catch a thing. Didn't even get a bite. We were totally frustrated as we could see the Lake Trout swimming beneath us in this small lake or really an over-sized pond. We kept at it for hours, until The Proud One said, "I've had enough."

So much for our big fishing excursion. So we looked around a bit and sure enough here in the wilderness, on a big lake, was a mansion and a couple of float planes out front. Like I said, The Proud One said the owner of the Argos at the time owned this mansion. The Proud One also said, the small lake or pond we were on, was supposed to be regularly stocked.

We headed back, down the old logging trail, car getting scraped to rat shit, and who knows doing what to the undercarriage.

When we got back, anybody who asked how we did, we gave a non-committal answer to. It was a lot of fun, but we didn't even get a bite – and we were the Great White Fishermen!

POSTSCRIPT – The Proud One moved to Vancouver Island many years ago after meeting his wife. He now lives in Victoria and we talk on the phone every once in a while.

I haven't seen him in 20 years, but we remain very good friends.

~7~ Beauty and the Beast

Now those good folks who read my first book 'Talk Turkey With Urqey' will recall the Penis Envy chapter. That's where The Quirky Guy placed his penis on The Bald Guy's shoulder, as The Bald Guy was phoning the Aurora Tigers' coach who was just fired, but didn't know it.

The following is how The Bald Guy got back at The Quirky Guy for that little episode. Now you must remember that back in the late 1970s and early 1980s, newspapers were a lot more fun to work at. You used a typewriter, for example, the paper came out once a week and you didn't have to worry about the Internet. It wasn't invented yet. Yes, we had a great deal of fun at The Newmarket Era and Express. Way too much fun. Way too much time on our hands.

So The Bald Guy gets this great idea. The Quirky guy is lonely – he wants to meet a woman – so he places a personal advertisement in The Toronto Star. The big mistake The Quirky Guy makes is that he tells everyone he put in this advertisement. A perfect opportunity for The Bald Guy opens up with a little imagination.

The Bald guy decided he'll write in and answer The Quirky Guy's advertisement. I mean The Bald Guy lays it on thick about this lonely, lonely woman, who lives in Newmarket, and how desperate she is to meet a real man. I'm still a bit hesitant to acknowledge this, but I go into the old Era photo files, which were quite extensive. Remember this is way before digital cameras, so everything was printed on photo paper and kept in case it was needed.

I find a former beauty queen modeling for the camera. She is quite beautiful. An old black and white photo about three inches by three inches. The Bald Guy decides to use on his 'love' letter the phone number of a girl who is the head of composing. Let's call her Blondie.

The Bald Guy gets an envelope, addresses it to The Star's personal box number, encloses the letter complete with Blondie's phone number and the photo I had picked out. It was quite the package. He stuck it in the mail and we both had a good laugh and just waited for snail mail to do its thing.

Three days later, the letter arrived for The Quirky Guy. And The Quirky Guy goes absolutely crazy with love for this new girl, I think The Bald Guy called her Priscilla. The Quirky Guy is dancing around the office and he's over the moon. Everybody he sees, he shows the letter and photo and says this is a match made in heaven. The Quirky Guy is salivating with excitement.

The Quirky Guy then shows the letter and photo to Blondie. Now Blondie who had a mouth like a trucker, reads the letter right to the end and exclaims, "That's my goddamn phone number. What the hell is going on?"

In that moment, the gig is up for The Bald Guy. The Quirky Guy's world comes crashing down with a huge thud. Now he's in one foul mood. "Who would dare do this?"

The Bald Guy and myself were having quite the laugh at The Quirky Guy's expense for about an hour while he pranced around the office showing off his love letter and beauty photo. We both knew we were in deep shit now.

As it turned out, it helped frustrate The Quirky Guy, who you'll read more of, in the next chapter.

POSTSCRIPT – I'm not sure the Editor-in-Chief ever knew about this little prank The Bald Guy and myself pulled. I can tell you we sure had a laugh. Such were the shenanigans at The Era prior to the advent of the Internet.

I can assure you that it's all work there now.

In today's politically correct workplace, you'd be fired for such a stunt now.

~8~ Poke her? I hardly know her!

In this politically correct world we live in today, a lot of what we did back when I started working would get a person fired. For example, you'll soon read about the 'Penny Incident' – definitely grounds to be dismissed.

In the previous chapter you read about how mean The Bald Guy and I were to The Quirky Guy, sending a response to his 'personal' ad in The Star. What you are about to read next, is just what happened to The Quirky Guy and it's quite a tale.

The Era was located next to The Beer Store on Charles Street, which wasn't the greatest location for us beer drinkers. Every Friday night we would buy a small case of beer and The Bald Guy, The Quirky Guy, Little Jimmy and myself would gather around one side of my 'T' shaped desk and play poker and have a few pints.

This went on for a long time. We just waited for the place to clear out on a Friday night and play for a couple of hours. It wasn't big stakes – we didn't make much money back then – but it was a lot of fun.

I don't know what exactly happened; The Quirky Guy was to say the least, a bit different. You might say off the wall. One day the Editor-in-Chief spied him out his window trying to smash his head on the windshield of his car. So the ambulance was called.

Next thing you know, The Quirky Guy is sent to the 6th floor of

York County Hospital.

The 6th floor was reserved for those with questionable mental states. Need I say more?

So The Quirky Guy is in there for quite a while. He phoned the odd time to say he was having a great time with all the females in the psych ward. And, he wanted a game of poker. You see, he said he'd be in there for a while.

So, like we used to do, The Bald Guy, Little Jimmy, Big Jim (head of composing) and myself went up to the 6th floor common room with a deck of cards. It was a bit difficult playing poker for money in the hospital – every time an orderly came near us, we had to throw a towel over the small coffee table to hide the cards and money.

Funny thing was, The Quirky Guy acted quite normal. We went up to play poker twice before he was released and everyone acted just normal – like it was being held on the corner of my desk.

And The Quirky Guy eventually came back to his job as Newmarket reporter at The Era. The Bald Guy moved to Mississauga to work and Little Jimmy got a job in Toronto. Big Jim eventually went to Mississauga too and I moved on to become News Editor of The Richmond Hill Liberal.

Like I said off the top, these were wild times – before political correctness shut down everything. Now it's an offence to say "Merry Christmas" – you have to say "Happy Holidays." And as I said, a lot of what we got up to – like drinking in the office – would today get us all fired.

But you know what, we all worked six days a week, most of us pulling an all-nighter each week and we cared about our product – The Newmarket Era. I reminisce fondly about all that talent.

POSTSCRIPT – I haven't heard or seen The Quirky Guy in many years. He did call me when I worked at a paper owned by Frank Stronach, looking for a job. He was back in Newmarket, but like I said, that was about 25 years ago.

The Bald Guy is back living in Newmarket.

The Editor-in-Chief is also residing in Newmarket.

~9~ Smoke anyone?

Back in 1977 when I was Sports Editor at The Newmarket Era and Express, I used to cover the Newmarket Flyers Junior A hockey team each Thursday night for their home games. The Flyers were owned by Mayor Ray Twinney and Dr. John Cole.

Twinney and Cole stood just inside the glass, where it was warm and I stood near there where the Zamboni came out. Back then Sports Editors had to take their own photos and this was the best spot for those 'goal' photos.

This was in the old Newmarket arena, now on Doug Duncan Drive, in honour of that man who worked at the arena all his life. It's now Riverwalk Commons and the Lions Hall. But I have a heck of a lot of memories from that old building watching Junior A hockey.

Back then, Junior A was the stepping stone to the Majors and then the NHL. It was a rough, tough and tumble league – everybody fighting to get up the hockey ladder. Gretzky was in this loop. I saw him play a few times back then. Aurora and Newmarket also had some very tough, feisty games with an enthusiastic crowd from both Aurora and Newmarket. That's an understatement, by the way.

But this one particular night, and I think it was between Newmarket and Aurora – fierce Yonge St. rivals – all hell broke loose. There was a bad infraction in the play, fights broke out between all the players on the ice and then the benches emptied. It was a full-scale donny-brook.

The ref and linesmen were just standing around. The police were called and about 30 uniformed officers showed up. The referee and linesmen were trying to get all the players into their dressing rooms so tempers could cool. That was right where I was standing, up from the ice, behind the glass.

I was having a field day taking great fight pictures, taking notes of who was fighting who, then while leaning over the glass, my pack of cigarettes fell out on the ice.

Well, much to my disbelief, the referee, who was standing there with little to do, until they all tired themselves out throwing punches, reached down, picked up my cigarettes and handed them up to me and said, "here you go." I thought, "how cool is that." All hell was breaking loose.

So the players try to exit the ice, right where most of the fans are sitting. Punches are still being thrown. The police try to cordon off the exit area. This is making for great photos! Then the fans get into it with the players and you thought all hell broke out before, now there was pandemonium. Police, fans and players all getting into it.

Finally, the players were locked in their respective dressing rooms. Some fans were taken away for a night in a cell, and the game was called – it wasn't going to continue this night. The police escorted the visiting team out of the arena, into their team bus, and right out of town, with lights flashing.

Those were the good old days in Newmarket. You don't see the likes of that mayhem anymore. But I got some really good pho-tos….made for a hell of a sports section that week.

POSTSCRIPT – Mayor Ray Twinney, as mentioned, also owned The Newmarket Rays, the men's fastball team in town, which eventually won the Canadian championship.

Dr. John Cole eventually became an MP for a term.

That old arena was torn down years ago.

Twinney has passed away, but Dr. Cole is still around.

~10~ A spider tale

Back in the heyday of The Newmarket Era and Express, things were a little crazy.

We had Dave Haskell as Publisher, a former Telegram man. He liked to hang out at The Compass Restaurant, which used to be located in Newmarket Plaza, for lunch every day with some of the town's finest citizens.

Needless to say, there wasn't much activity from Dave's front after lunch.

We had a Coke machine that gave you a Coke for a quarter – one of those old ones where the bottles were on ice and they were standing straight up. You pushed the one you paid for to the opening. We also had a coffee and hot chocolate machine. For 20 cents you could get one of the most God-awful coffees ever made. But myself, and all the other reporters and editors lived on this stuff. I think it also had a soup button, so that shows just how old that was. It was 1976 and I just graduated from Ryerson with a degree in Journalism.

Dave Haskell would never have managed without Ethel Wall – my dear old Ethel Wall. As I'm writing this, she is 92-years-young. We were in the old Era building on Charles Street, right next to The Beer Store. Ethel, who was the head accountant and Girl Friday (she took care of just about everything), was in the office next to Dave. Dave was in the middle, the Editor-in-Chief was next to the north and Ethel was next to Dave on the south. All in offices with that old paneling that people used to put in their basement, with sliding windows between all the offices.

Ethel, for some reason, had an old door that wasn't used, out to the where the reporters sat, including me. I always listened in the winter as Ethel would come in, sit at her desk and take off her winter boots and put on office shoes. She did this every morning like clockwork.

My wife and I used to work all night to get the paper out on Tuesdays for delivery Wednesdays. I was Sports Editor and she was Photographer. I now don't know why, but we were the only two that used to pull all-nighters. (We weren't married at the time, but you can see what develops in the Dark Room!!)

So it was at one of these all-nighters that I got a brilliant idea. I planned it for weeks in advance. I needed some special tools – like a real-life, look-alike Tarantula (spider) with real fur, some fishing line and voila, my plan would be almost complete.

One late night, I tied the fishing line to a leg of the Tarantula. I placed the Tarantula in one of Ethel's office shoes, and ran the fishing line out, under the door that was never used, to my desk. And I waited for Ethel to come in to work.

Well, Ethel came in at her usual 8:30 a.m. There wasn't much action in the newsroom where I sat, but a full composing staff and front office staff were in.

I heard Ethel sit down and take off her winter boots. Then I just lightly tugged at the fishing line to make the Tarantula wiggle a bit.

Well, dear readers, you wouldn't have believed the earth-shattering scream that came out of Ethel's mouth. Behind her office wall, I was crying tears of laughter. I was almost doubled over in fits of laughter. I still thank my lucky stars that neither Dave nor the Editor-in-Chief were in yet.

I talked with Ethel recently and she said she stomped on that Tarantula, not realizing that it was a fuzzy replica, trying to kill the beast.

But in my memory, I know that Ethel knew it was me. She followed the fish line after she had settled down and let me have it. And to this day, I know I deserved it!!

POSTSCRIPT – As I mentioned Ethel is 92-years-young at the time of writing.

Dave Haskell is long gone.

The Editor-in-Chief still lives in Newmarket.

~11~ Dr. Suzuki, a God, or
left-wing zealot?

"Sanctified air."

That's apparently what you share when you are in the presence of Dr. David Suzuki.

My God, did I actually write that? Sanctified air? Do we actually have a Canadian personality, a television personality, the founder of a foundation, the writer of a weekly column in many community newspapers, who actually thinks that to be around him is to breathe in 'sanctified air'?

As comedian Steve Martin would say, and did say on Saturday Night Live so many years ago, "weeellll, exxxcuse meeee."

And that's not all, folks. Apparently Dr. Suzuki likes to be surrounded by females to serve as 'bodyguards'.

But I first need to set the stage. To give a one-hour talk, Dr. Suzuki billed John Abbott College in Montreal $30,000, plus expenses. Add in his airline ticket, his $841 hotel room, a photographer and other costs, the total hit to this small, publicly-funded school was $41,640.

I guess if you are breathing in 'sanctified air' all the time, you also need a photographer. I don't know. "You're So Vain," by Carly Simon comes to mind.

Thanks to Jonathan Kay of the National Post and Sun News TV, through the access-to-information request, Sun Network discovered e-mails that reveal the odd requests Dr. Suzuki made in regard to his 2012 visit to Montreal.

One of the university officials reported to her colleagues as follows:

"We have learned via Dr. Suzuki's assistant, that although the Dr. does not like to have bodyguards per se, he does not mind having a couple of ladies (females) that would act as bodyguards in order that he may travel from one venue to another without being accosted too many times along the way. Why females you ask? Well, he is a male. No seriously, I believe it is his way of being discreet and less intimidating."

According to Kay, college officials discussed the dress of these "female bodyguards," then this e-mail: "In terms of acknowledging their contribution after the tours are completed, we will need to gather (the ladies) together at the end to either give them some brief time with Suzuki (which) I will try to make happen, either by having them step out of the penthouse or enabling them to join the group in the sanctified air."

I applaud Ezra Levant of Sun News TV who has been going after this left-wing CBC personality for weeks. Somewhere, in this great land of ours, someone has to speak out.

It appalls me that no one at the college spoke out about this sexist 'rider' on Dr. Suzuki's arrival and talk. Not a word. They even helped in the selection of the female students.

January 30 of this year, John Abbott released a statement, so I leave it up to you to decide for yourselves:

"To set the record straight regarding Dr. Suzuki's visit to our campus Oct. 24, both male and female students escorted him throughout a full day and evening of activities in order to facilitate his movements throughout our campus. Those students, all of whom were chosen for their professionalism, were part of our Police Technology program. There was no rider in Dr. Suzuki's contract specifying the gender or dress code of those assisting him throughout the day. The negative comments and innuendos made are demeaning to those students and to the College and are the result of the misinterpretation of e-mails exchanged between colleagues."

Sounds a bit too good to be true to me. Deny everything and it'll go away. Much like Senator Mike Duffy did until he realized the media really did have the goods on him. The John Abbott statement, just for the record, made no mention of the 'sanctified air' reference, which has infuriated me beyond belief – how dare a human being put himself above Godliness!

POSTSCRIPT – The above column I printed in Voice of the Farmer a few years ago.

I sent a copy to the local newspaper, but they chose not to run it

~12~ Your thoughts for a penny?

Those were heady days, back in 1976, when I started at The Newmarket Era and Express as Sports Editor.

My first day, they gave me a desk, a rotary telephone, a typewriter, some paper and a company issue ashtray. Needless to say, I started my smoking career. We all smoked in the newsroom in those days. Editor-in-Chief TC didn't venture into the newsroom too much. He didn't smoke and all I can remember about those days was a constant cloud of smoke hovering over the newsroom.

The newsroom, in the Charles Street building in Newmarket beside the old Beer Store made for some interesting times. Our old publisher was an alcoholic who kept a bottle of vodka in the back of the toilet. When he felt like a drink, he just went to the washroom.

There were about five of us in the newsroom. BM was our News Editor, located off to the side and beside the office of TC. BM didn't smoke either, now that I think about it. Needless to say, we were one rowdy bunch in the newsroom … all guys, with the exception of my future wife, Aase, who was the photographer and spent most of her time in the darkroom processing film – black and white and colour.

The lunch room was at the back of the building, just off the composing area. So most of the staff would walk through the newsroom to the lunch room and most of the time were easy targets for our shenanigans.

We had these solid cover calendar books issued to us and for some strange reason, we started throwing a penny in the air and smacking it hard with our calendar book at each other. God knows we could have easily taken an eye or two out. This went on for weeks until one day, Ethel Wall, our accountant, who we all loved dearly, was making her way to the lunchroom.

Well, to this day, I don't know what possessed me. I was age 21 and Ethel had to be age 50 or so, but I tossed a penny in the air and smacked it hard at Ethel's direction. Well, this illustrious penny caught Ethel in the forehead, about an inch from her eye. She immediately went down like a sack of potatoes.

MY GOD! I thought. I've killed her. She laid on the floor until Betty Bishop and I helped her up. And I saw a welt coming up where the penny hit. I thought to myself, "You idiot, what have you done?"

Well, Ethel knew she'd given me the scare of my life. The whole newsroom stopped and were all silent. We all took in what had just happened.

I definitely consoled my dear Ethel. She said in compensation for my dastardly deed, she wanted five pounds of Laura Secord chocolates, which I promptly bought the next day, had it wrapped and prepared a nice "sorry" card.

To this day, I think that if Dave the Publisher or TC, the Editor-in-Chief had known, I would have been fired on the spot. To this day, I am indebted to Ethel for not getting me fired. And believe me, that was the end of tossing a penny in the air and smacking it with our calendar book.

About a month later, Ethel admitted to the newsroom that she "pretended" to go down after getting hit. She said she had "faked" it to get me worried and get us to clean up our act in the newsroom. I really don't know. It's over 40 years later and to this day, I don't know if she "faked" it.

Years later Ethel asked me to say a few words about her at her funeral. She wanted me to tell the tale in Chapter 10 and also about the penny incident. I said I would, although it would be quite painful. Understand I love Ethel dearly and I thought I'd killed her.

Today, Ethel is 92-years-young and she said she no longer needs me to talk at her funeral. She said, "I just wanted to make you sweat for hitting me with that penny."

POSTSCRIPT – as written in Chapter 10, Publisher Dave is long gone.

TC lives in Newmarket and BM lives in Richmond Hill.

The Newmarket Era and Express changed its name to The Era-Banner and then back to just The Era.

I've since retired from the newspaper business after 40 years writing and editing and I credit my strong ethics (despite the penny incident) to TC, who was a stern, but fair Editor and really knows his English. He's published a number of books as well.

~13~ What a start to a New Year

Ahh, what one gets up to when they are young. And it's fun to look back, which is what this book is about.

Back in 1979, I was South Shore Editor of The Era, which was its edition to cover Keswick, Sutton, Jackson's Point and Pefferlaw. It was a lot of fun back then and all the media covering Georgina council had a great relationship.

I had organized several hockey matches between the local media and the council and staff of the day. We played these games in all the arenas in Georgina. Bob Johnston, the Editor of The Advocate and his paper's owner Harry Stemp all played for the media. (In one game Harry brought in a Maple Leafs player for the media and we won a lop-sided affair at Sutton Arena). Bob was our goalie. Chris Knowles, the Sports Editor at the Aurora Banner was a forward, along with myself. There were others to make up the media team.

But back in 1979, after many media-council hockey games, their Facilities Manager Fred Horvath, who was council's goalie and a great goalie at that, organized a game for January 1, New Year's Day 1980, to be played on Lake Simcoe. That's right, outdoors on Lake Simcoe, as a fund-raiser for some local charity.

The game was promoted heavily in all the newspapers and on CKVR, who always sent a player to play in these games. The game was set for 2 p.m. on January 1, 1980. (Somewhere in my closet, I have a five-minute Super 8 film capturing this event).

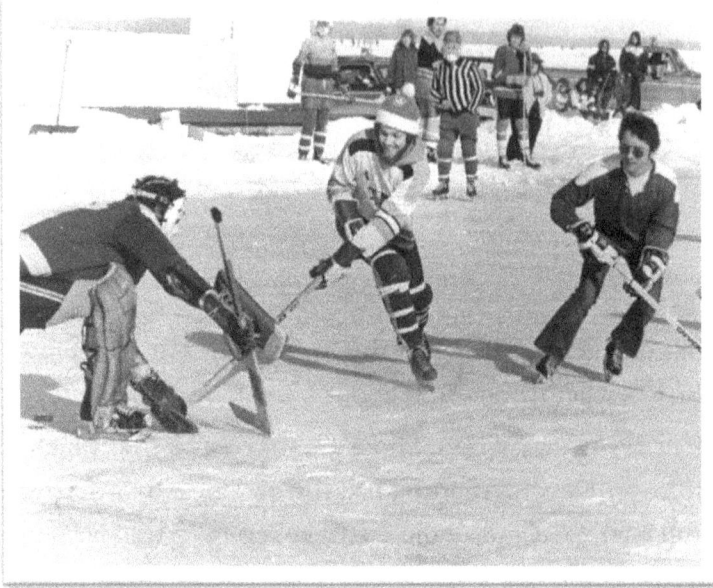

The author scores on Town Council Goalie Fred Horvath.
In the background is The Bald Guy (with hair); Banner
Sports Editor at the time Chris Knowles and behind him,
Banner Reporter Carol Mulligan.
Photo by Aase Urquhart

Fred really outdid himself. He thought of everything, right down to the smallest detail. We all met at the former Irish House (which at the time was a media hangout) to get into our hockey gear. We arrived at noon and the bar's owner Johnny put us all downstairs to get changed.

I remember being simply amazed at the time, but Fred arranged for a school bus to pick us up and take us to a cleared hockey rink on Lake Simcoe in Jackson's Point. When the bus arrived, there were already about 200 spectators. Fred had arranged for bleachers to be brought in and placed just on shore.

The game lasted about 60 minutes, with three 20-minute periods and we played with a tennis ball and puck – out on Lake Simcoe in the middle of winter. It was a cold, but sunny day and council and the media just had a blast, as the crowd roared with every goal. Yes, we had nets frozen into the ice and referees, even painted lines on the ice.

Council won that game, thanks to the outstanding goal-tending of Fred, and a large trophy was presented to the council team out on the ice. (Somewhere in the basement of the Civic Centre is a large trophy that then mayor Joe Dales purchased himself just for these media-council hockey games). My future wife, Aase, was on hand to take photos of the memorable event for The Era. (An excellent photo is included in this book). Carol Mulligan was there taking photos for The Banner. The Bald Guy was there, I think he played defense.

It was just a great day and good way to bring in the New Year and new decade. For, it was shortly after that I was appointed News Editor of The Richmond Hill Liberal and then Editor-in-Chief.

After the game, this school bus took us back to The Irish House, where we changed into street clothes and went upstairs for a cocktail or two with all our girlfriends and wives and most of council and their staff. It was just a great end to a wonderful day. A couple of drinks, talk about the game, and just share some New Year good cheer with our rosy red cheeks.

I really don't remember how much we raised for charity, but I gotta admit, Fred Horvath did an outstanding job. Now a Facilities Manager would be scrutinized for wasting taxpayers' dollars!! How the times have changed.

POST SCRIPT – As mentioned somewhere in this book, Bob Johnston passed away some years ago of cancer, and I think all of Georgina misses Bob. He went on to become mayor for two terms.

Harry Stemp eventually sold his newspaper holdings. I don't know what happened to him.

Chris Knowles was a very good friend of mine and I haven't seen or heard from him in years.

Carol Mulligan ended up in Sudbury and I haven't spoken to her in about 30 years.

~14~ No theatre in town
has me seeing 'red'

What has happened to the arts community in northern York Region?

Other than the odd Shakespeare outdoor production at the Sharon Temple or Fairy Lake in Newmarket, there is little going on this summer. The acts appearing at the Stephen Leacock Theatre in Keswick really don't appeal to me. I want live theatre.

York Region can build new roadways, implement a full transit system, put up red light cameras, but what has the regional municipality done for the arts? In Georgina they spent millions creating a ski hill and operating it.

But what about rebuilding Canada's oldest summer stock theatre, which burnt to the ground a few years ago mysteriously? Yes, I'm talking about the famed Red Barn Theatre. Over its more than 60 years of existence, it saw famous actors from around the globe, even more famous artistic directors and set designers.

Going to the Red Barn Theatre in Jackson's Point was always an 'event' – it was more than just live theatre. It was always a memorable experience.

As theatre critic for The Era in the late 1970s to early 2000s, I personally took in many, many memorable performances, from Tom Kneebone in Cabaret, to seeing politicians of the day perform on stage thanks to Peter Gzowski, to the very special performances when Ernie Swartz was artistic director and director.

It was under Ernie in the early 1980s I took in the absolute best performance of 'Dracula' – complete with live bats flying about the Barn – a costly production, but deemed a highlight of the Red Barn's existence. I remember seeing Larry Solway, the Nylons' first concert, and attending a fundraiser held by the late Whipper Billy Watson – a champion of so many causes in York Region.

Really, without the Red Barn, which attracted theatre-goers and bus loads from all around southern Ontario to the shores of Lake Simcoe, Georgina Town Council is (excuse the pun) missing the boat. The Red Barn brought in many tourist dollars to the area.

The Red Barn was a 'business', Georgina mayor and councillors are always saying how the town needs to grow, needs business, so they put in another highway – 404. But nothing for the arts. I understand Georgina has a Business Development Office with full-time staff.

How about pursuing the resurrection of the Red Barn Theatre on its former lands? How about working with the Lake Simcoe Arts Foundation, the old Red Barn Foundation, the Georgina Arts Centre, and whomever else wants to get involved in this very, very worthy project to rejuvenate a stale Georgina?

POSTSCRIPT – this column ran in The Newmarket Era in September, 2014.

~15~ Where's the theatre act?

Both Georgina and Newmarket have grown extensively over the years. Many years ago, both thriving communities had an active live theatre scene.

I have seen many plays at the former Newmarket Town Hall, now under construction, with many different theatre groups. Years ago, there was even a summer stock theatre company in there that put on some great plays. And don't forget the plays in the 1970s by Artistic Director Paul Aspland, who even appeared in the first Star Wars movie

Today, the Newmarket Theatre on Mulock just doesn't get that much live theatre. Neither does the Stephen Leacock Theatre in Keswick. Usually just Yuk Yuk's comedians or music impersonators.

But years ago, I'm talking in the 1970s and 1980s, the South Shore Little Theatre was a thriving troupe of actors and actresses (non-politically correct, I know).

I can remember many times former Georgina Advocate Editor Bob Johnston (now deceased) and myself (The Era's South Shore Editor) would be invited to the Belhaven Hall for the final dress rehearsal of a play by the South Shore Little Theatre to do a review for our upcoming issue of their latest offering.

The South Shore Little Theatre, which for some strange reason changed its name in the 1990s to South Shore Theatre, put on some great English farce, English comedies and pantomimes – pre-the Norm Foster playwright days.

And it was all in the intimate Belhaven Hall, prior to Whipper Billy Watson and fund-raising chair Bob Garden building the Stephen Leacock Theatre. Man About Town (a young) John McLean took the tickets and sometimes performed. My favourite actors from those early days were Joe and Jackie Diasio – they were simply wonderful! They had comic timing down perfectly.

In later years the South Shore Little Theatre moved to the new Thrush theatre at the Stephen Leacock Theatre. I haven't heard of them for years. They put on performances there along with the Queensville Players.

With all the growth in Newmarket and Georgina, with all these new residents, have theatre groups become passé? I don't know, sometimes I think we're a society of iPhone users and television watchers.

Last week I met a delightful young girl, Alex Karolyi who created Shadow Path Theatre Productions. Alex, who lives in Newmarket, organizes Plays in Cafes – there were three in the final week of September alone. On October 30th, there's a Murder Mystery – part of the Cuisine Scenes she runs, at Hungry Brew Hops on Main Street Newmarket. (Go to www.shadowpaththeatre.ca)

I plan on taking in some of Alex's theatre productions. And by the way, Georgina is not the same community without the effervescent Bob Johnston, a larger than life character who became mayor of that great town for two terms.

POSTSCRIPT – The above column ran in The Era late September, 2014.

~16~ The couch affair

You know back in the old days, when you were a kid, you did some pretty dumb and stupid things.

My parents bought a modest bungalow the year after I was born, in 1955. They had lived in Toronto for the first year of my life. I don't really remember the move, but just prior to my mother passing away, she told me when I was age two and a half, a Polish couple with a little boy my age moved into this new subdivision in Richmond Hill.

My Mom told me I constantly hung around with this neighbour, playing outside, and I astounded my parents by talking fluent Polish at such a young age.

A few years later, Big Ad was born and then came along Tracy. That's where this tale begins when Big Ad was about age seven, I would have been age 10 and Tracy around age four – a very tender age. As three children, we got along famously, but being a boy, I was known to get into a lot of trouble. Yes, I got into a lot of trouble and usually was rewarded with a spanking with my Dad's belt.

In this modest bungalow, we had an old small, black and white television, a huge living room rug, some lamps and this massive burgundy couch. For some strange reason, Big Ad and I used to take delight in standing on the edge of this really, really comfortable old couch and jumping on the cushions. One day, we got the brilliant idea to roll youngest sister Tracy up in the living room carpet, then place her in the middle of the couch and then standing on the edge of the couch and take turns jumping on the buried Tracy.

Now I don't know the ramifications of such an action – I'll let Tracy tell you in the next chapter – but it was a helluva lot of fun. Big Ad and I had the time of our lives! Best thing about it, we didn't get caught. I can't imagine what the punishment for almost killing Tracy would have been. I don't remember, but we must have bribed Tracy with something.

Years later, Tracy noted that she almost asphyxiated in that carpet rolled tight around her and us jumping on her. I remember, it went on for some time before we let poor Tracy out of her carpet prison.

Ahh, the memories of youth! Sometimes we just got up to some real tomfoolery. Like I said off the top, not the brightest of childhood games.

I sincerely hope it didn't scar Tracy for life or anything like that!

POSTSCRIPT – The next chapter will be Tracy's recount of those events mentioned above.

~17~ Tracy's chapter in response to couch jumping

By Tracy Campbell
Rod's youngest sister

Scarred? Who wouldn't be? And that wasn't the worst of it! It was brutal growing up with a brother six years older than I.

As a toddler, the first sentence I ever uttered was "roddydidit," which became my mantra until I was silenced under the blanket (it wasn't a carpet and my brother forgot to mention that he tied it over me with my own skipping rope before putting me under the couch cushions). I believe I was around 30 years old before he could come near me without trying to hide from him exclaiming, "Can't breathe, can't breathe, can't breathe."

Once this familial terrorist said he had a fun idea and asked me to sit on his feet as he lay on his back on the floor with his knees bent to his chest. I sat down and Roddy kicked his legs as hard as he could. I first had the wind knocked out of me when I hit the ceiling!! And then again when I smashed down onto the floor. There were no bribes so that I wouldn't squeal to our parents. I do remember him deviously spending his spare time collecting blackmail material on my sister and I.

And he was physically much bigger than we were which made it easy for him to threaten to "beat us up" if we ever snitched.

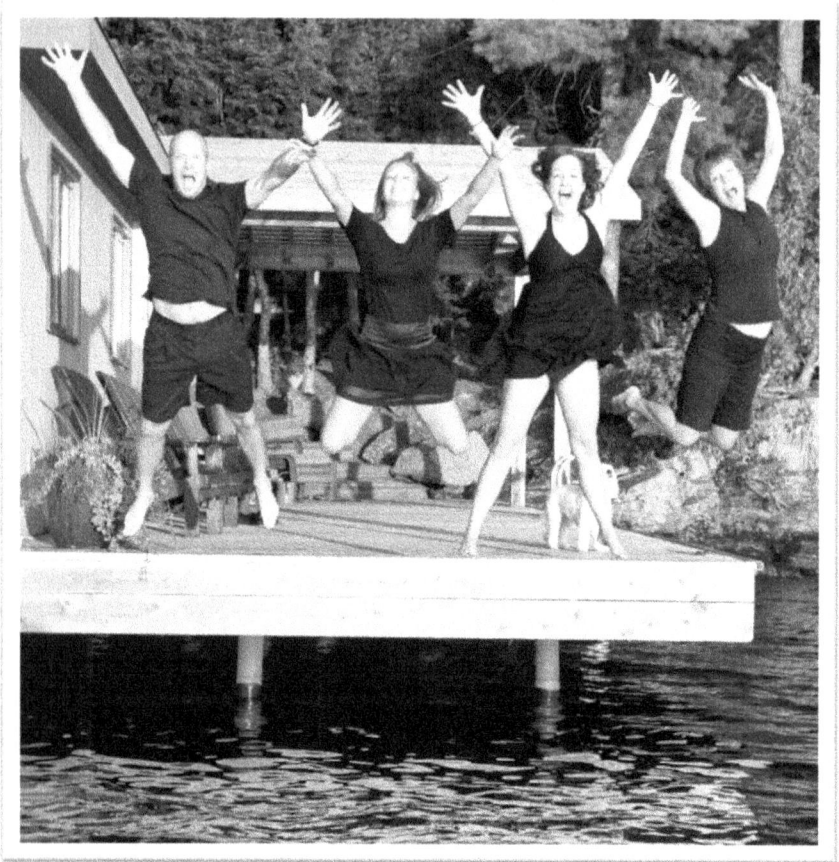

This is the Campbell family at their cottage. As you can see, Tracy turned out fine and the 'Kids are Alright', not to mention her husband also.

Photo courtesy of Kelly Holinshead of Shutterbug Gallery in Hunstville, Ontario.

As a child I enjoyed drawing and playing with my dolls in my room, but Roddy enjoyed having a fun toy to torment. Memories of my childhood were fraught with him sitting on my head as I tried to watch TV; hugging for dear life tethered to my mother's leg for protection; black eyes from being forced to play back catcher or goalie (because really I was...a target); being humiliated as my siblings played monkey in the middle with my diary laughing uproariously as they read excepts, or being terrified from them jumping out at me from every shadow in our house. But the worst fate I endured as the "baby" in the family was when they took my treasured Chatty Cathy doll that I toted everywhere and threw her against the wall. She never spoke again.

When I got older, my bullying brother decided it was more delightful to intimidate boys who mustered up the courage to ask Ad or I out. In those days, which would have been about 1976, when the only phone in your household rang (which was attached to the wall...and ours was a party line) all the kids in the family would dart for it hoping the call would be for them. The very first young suitor to ever call our house for me had the unfortunate luck of having my brother beat us all to the phone. Instead of being polite and handing the phone over to me, he asked the young lad if he was really 'sure' he wanted to speak to me. That was enough for the poor lad to hang up and I never even found out who it was (we didn't have call display then either).

The pinnacle of his campaign happened on a day when I first brought a boy home. Everyone else was out and wouldn't you know who arrived home unexpectedly. Hearing Rod coming in the door, I quickly hid my friend in a downstairs closet and acted like I was home alone. Somehow Rod, like most controlling rulers, quickly suspected what was going on and stomped all over the house yelling, "Fee, Fi, Fo Fum....I smell the blood of a scrawny little BUM!". Trembling in fear as he hid in the dark closet, by the time Rod marched down the stairs, swung the closet door open and exposed my 80 lb. pre-pubescent paramour, I think one could smell something else!

People think it is great growing up the youngest and getting all the 'attention'. HA! Who wants that kind of attention? If I was scarred it only drove me to want to be bigger, better, smarter, stronger, taller, more talented, faster, go further....and say to myself, "I'll show them!". I'm not sure if I succeeded but now somehow, unbelievably, my brother Rod is my best friend.

~18~ The drinks

Russell the Rascal, as my sister Tracy calls my now deceased Dad, was quite a character.

For example, he never missed a garage sale – cutting out the listings in the newspaper, visiting every one and picking up what he thought were great deals. Living through the Great Depression will do that to you. He often outfitted himself with garage sale clothes.

But this isn't about the summer when garage sales happen. This is about our Christmas Day celebration, complete with turkey, stuffing and mashed potatoes, not to mention a slew of vegetables. It was back when both my parents were around. They were getting older and my mother always was a bit frantic cooking up such a mess of food.

My sister had a family by then, I was long-since married and Adrienne had a steady boyfriend. We all gathered at my Mom and Dad's on Christmas Day to have a delicious turkey dinner and then retire later to the living room, with the Christmas tree and all the presents to open.

Prior to us arriving, we found out later, that my Mom had put my Dad in charge of drinks. My Mom insisted he do this as she was preparing this lavish Christmas dinner.

So we all arrive about 5 p.m. My Mom and Dad always ate at 6 p.m., like clockwork. So we sit down in the big living room and after my Mom says hello and retired back to the kitchen, she says, "Russ, the drinks!"

So my Dad gets talking, mostly to myself and Tracy's husband Richard, mostly about old stories growing up in Swansea.

My mother leans out the kitchen door and says, "Russ, the drinks."

So we've been there about 40 minutes and still no drinks nor a sign of a drink to come. Russell the Rascal is still gabbing up a storm, not a care in the world, reminiscing about his youth, what it was like to be young.

My Mom comes right out of the kitchen, taps him on the shoulder and says, "Russell the drinks," and retires to the kitchen.

So it's just about time for dinner. I can hear my Mom putting plates of food on the large dining room table. I can tell my Mom has had enough. She storms back into the living room and screams at my father, "Russell the drinks!!!!"

My Dad stops in mid-conversation, looks at my mother, and says, "Okay, damn it, I'll have a Rum and Coke," and carries on talking.

We all killed ourselves laughing at Russell the Rascal. And yes, we did get drinks in time for dinner. I think Richard made them.

POST SCRIPT – Richard relayed this complete story at the Celebration of Life for my Dad, who was two weeks shy of his 90th birthday when he passed away.

In fact, Richard gave quite the memorable talk that day and I thank him. He has many fond memories of my Dad.

My late Mom and Dad, Lucille and Russell, in this undated photo dressed as a Saloon Girl and Sheriff for a function they were attending.

Submitted photo

~19~ Grey Cup fumes

Years ago, I was Editor of the Georgina Era-Banner. It doesn't exist anymore after Metroland bought the Georgina Advocate, where I ended up with my old friend John Slykhuis.

The office of the Georgina Era-Banner was in the basement of Paul Connors house. Paul was the Advertising Director and a great guy. He's no longer in the newspaper business, he's running a very successful music shop with his sons and daughter.

Now in this basement, there was one washroom. It was small and just inside Paul's workshop. It was a sprawling basement with many rooms and many people working there. At one time we had Paul and three sales reps, two telemarketers and a receptionist, plus myself. We all had to share this one washroom, with no air vent.

It was right after the Grey Cup, the next day in fact. I am a big Argo fan and this was back in the Doug Flutie years. These were the only years that Aase ever watched my beloved Argos with me, because she had a crush on the quarterback, Doug Flutie.

Argos were in the Grey Cup that year and I was destined to have a Grey Cup Party, which I certainly did. I prepared my world-famous chili for everyone – one big pot of cooking, very hot chili, plus lots of breads to cool down the mouth. I also had lots of cold beer on hand. I had about 18 people over.

The Argos won the Grey Cup that year and everyone had their fill of chili – not so hot you can't eat it, but just hot enough to leave a burning sensation in your mouth – and lots of beer. Yes, we had designated drivers when it all ended.

The next day at my office at Paul Connors' basement, I remember, it was around 10 a.m., I felt that familiar rumbling in my stomach. Finally, three bowls of very spicy chili, bread and beer were catching up with me. I headed to that rather small bathroom off the workshop area.

Not to gross you out and get into specifics, but I definitely defecated and felt very relieved. Although this was now late November, so no windows were open and no fan in the bathroom. And again not to gross you out, it left quite the odour. Something had died in that bathroom.

So I head back to my tiny office just off the main foyer. One of the sales reps, whose office was closest to the bathroom, her name was Irene, starts sneezing and exclaims in a loud voice, "It smells like dog shit in here! Did someone let a dog in?"

Then the receptionist Sherry pipes up, "Yes, I smell it. It does smell like dog shit." Then pandemonium in the office – everyone says they can smell dog shit – I mean everyone and they are looking around for the 'dog.'

Well, I have tears streaming down my face – I'm thinking, they think it's a dog!!! They think some dog shit in here!! Oh boy, I was laughing so hard, I had to shut my door so they wouldn't know that the real culprit was me.

After Irene sprayed the office with some scented spray, the smell went away, but boy, for about 10 minutes there, I was having the laugh of my life. The office shut down about a year later and they never put two and two together and figured out it was my bowel movement. But I knew!

POST SCRIPT – *As mentioned Paul operates a music shop with his sons and daughter.*

Susie was my photographer at the time and is mentioned in this book.

Unfortunately, Irene died of cancer much too young.

I don't know whatever became of our receptionist Sherry.

~20~ We have it all wrong

You know, I'm a bit mystified. I simply can't understand our obsession with so-called celebrities.

A lot of them I don't know anymore. The old movie stars like Clark Cable, Carole Lombard, John Wayne, Marilyn Monroe, I know. But these new stars, I don't have a clue. Why is Lindsay Lohan in the news all the time – because she's a drug-abuser and alcoholic? Why do I need to know that?

I saw on the internet tonight when I turned on my computer that Tom Hanks collects old typewriters and Angeline Jolie likes something a little more dangerous, but it didn't say what. I could not care less. When I turn on my computer, I saw that some actress I've never heard of is wearing a dress that makes her look like a spider. I see that some actress is wearing shoes that make her feet look too big.

It's an upside-down world. We praise and idolize the completely wrong people. I really care more about compassion, first for single mothers. I've known many women through my years whose spouses have been idiots and left them to raise the children, earn a living doing so, and struggle through life. My heart goes out to single women. We should be singing their praises, not some recent movie star who earns millions for appearing on celluloid. I just don't get it.

And with the hockey season now upon us – and I know for a lot of couch potatoes, it's a sense of relaxation – but these hockey players earn millions and for what? Flying about North America playing a game they love and getting paid extravagant amounts of money. It's really a travesty.

The same for baseball players, whose season has ended and basketball players. That's only in North America; soccer players in England and Europe make huge sums of money, so do F1 drivers. It's much different in Europe, where people still go to the games and to see F1 races.

It's just a mixed up world. We idolize the wrong people. Everyday folk who get up at 4:30 to 5 every morning to feed the cattle, milk the cows or work the fields are the real heroes that make this country work.

Why don't we offer more praise for farmers and farm families? Hockey, NFL and baseball players, not to mention movie stars, that's just entertainment. Yes, we need entertainment, but why pay them vast sums of money?

I agree there is nothing like sitting down on a Saturday night to watch Hockey Night In Canada – I did it with my grandfather on my mother's side from age eight to about 15. Today, I love Don Cherry and Ron MacLean. (Don Cherry and Ron MacLean don't make vast sums of money working for CBC). (Rogers took over everything hockey after this rant was written).

But, it's pure entertainment. For Pete's Sake, you can go visit your local library and get more bang for your buck. The library has movies, CDs, DVDs and best of all, lots and lots of books.

Mary Macfarlane, who wrote for me is not only one very busy farm wife, but a nurse, and a heck of a writer, wrote a column recently in Voice of the Farmer, about how teenagers are too busy on the computer. They don't go outside. They don't read newspapers. They are inside getting a jailhouse tan. Man, that column almost made me cry.

No, I think Prime Minister Stephen Harper should announce a special award – like a Canadian Medal – each year to a bunch of outstanding farmers. Ordinary people who have made their communities better places to live in. That's way more important than if Lindsay Lohan is in rehab again.

POSTSCRIPT – I was editor of Voice of the Farmer for 18 years.

Mary Macfarlane, bless her heart, wrote for me for years and did a splendid job.

The above ran in Voice of the Farmer just before my departure.

~21~ A talk for Chris Campbell

When I was a young teenager, Chris Campbell was a sort of an icon at Richmond Hill High School. Although I went to Bayview High School, anybody who was anybody knew of Chris Campbell.

I used to venture over to Richmond Hill High School, mainly because it had all the hot babes. I remember going over once and Chris was playing his guitar in that very small gym, surrounded by his peers and classmates. Everyone seemed to be in awe of Chris.

On Yonge Street, close to the famed A&W hangout, there was a clubhouse of some kind. It was only for Richmond Hill students, it seemed. I became friends later with Joe Durante who went to Richmond Hill (all us long hairs used to hang out together) and went to that clubhouse once. The aura and presence of Chris was in that clubhouse.

Later in life, when Tracy was dating Richard, I used to go to the Richmond Inn downstairs and catch Chris with his band. It was always a memorable night. I'll never forget his large belt of harmonicas strung around his shoulder to his thigh – and man could he play those harmonicas. Really good music for the Richmond Inn. (Which later became a strip joint and was eventually shutdown and demolished).

When Chris, who was older than me, and I were growing up in Richmond Hill, it was the drug years. Timothy Leary had just introduced LSD to North America, pot was everywhere and organic mescaline was easily found. Yes, the police were quite active in those days.

Today kids sit in their bedroom and play video games. Go figure!

Many of us didn't make it through the drug years without some sort of casualty. 'Nuff said.

Even later in life, I actually had a chance with my university girlfriend to spend a night with Chris and Joanne in the Campbell basement. While Chris played the piano, Shelley, myself and Joanne sang all the rock and roll classics. We drank wine, we sang, we talked and we just had a great time.

And then, for the very first Moonshine Café Campbell Clan Concert, my wife, Aase, was the only one with an old Sony Camcorder who captured the concert on film. She was able to get Chris, in later years, singing three classic Van Morrison tunes before the power died. I watched that DVD recently and the hairs stick up on my neck from Chris' performance that night.

In closing I just want to say that two of my favourite people – Mary and Alex Campbell raised three wonderful sons, with Chris being the oldest, and instilled in them a love of music. That is so wonderful. If you've been to the Moonshine Café and other venues for the Campbell Concerts in aid of charity and you know how talented Brad and Richard are. Today, I hope Chris was a big influence in their decision to keep on with music.

Chris is in heaven now, and I know he will find peace there. He suffered terribly in later years and there comes a time to say goodbye. But we will miss him. God Bless everyone here tonight.

POSTSCRIPT – I wrote the above to say at the Celebration of Life for Chris Campbell (who died much too young) at the famed Moonshine Café in Oakville.

Mary, his mother, said to me recently, that she didn't know how he made it that long; he just wasn't that healthy in later years.

Chris died at his home in Stratford about two years ago at the time this book is published.

~22~ The Atari Affair

The year was 1984. Aase and I had been going out for about seven years and I decided to move in with her in Newmarket. I was Editor-in-Chief of the Richmond Hill Liberal at the time.

Now, Aase was lucky enough to get this fantastic apartment in a Century home on the Main Street of Newmarket. I think Big John said it was originally a Catholic Manse. It was a huge three-floor house, up on a hill. Aase was lucky enough to get this apartment thanks to Big John, who lived on the main floor and was caretaker/manager of the house. He also rented.

Aase had the second floor, which was really three bedrooms, but only two were used as bedrooms. The front room to the left, we used as a fancy dining room. It had a huge living room overlooking Main Street and a huge master bedroom with a huge bay window. The bathroom was also quite spacious. And the kitchen was bigger than my current house.

After I moved in, Big John and I became great friends, much to the dismay of his wife. I was definitely a bad influence. I had been chumming with Big John while dating Aase, but when I moved in, we became that much closer.

1983 was the time that one of the very first video game machines came out. They certainly weren't like the games of today. (A friend on the weekend told me that the video gaming industry earns more profit in

North America than the movie industry. That kind of blew me away).

I had purchased an Atari machine – one of two of the gaming systems that came out at that time. The other was Intelivision. It cost me over $200 for the Atari system and two games. A few months later they came out with 'better' games with 'better' graphics. So I bought these advanced Atari Football and Atari Baseball games. I also bought the Indy 500.

The author and Big John playing Atari late one night in 1984 in Aase's apartment on Main Street, Newmarket.

Photo by Aase Urquhart

Big John started to play these games with me and we had a helluva lot of fun. We got into it so much, I had my brother-in-law who worked in the city, go to the largest toy store in Toronto and buy these special Atari controllers (joysticks with no buttons like today) that were much more superior than what it came with.

After multiple games on this Atari system, I realized one of the controllers worked a little better than the other, so I marked the bottom with a small 'X'.

Now, this old house had copper pipes running from the main floor, up to Aase's apartment on the second floor, all the way to the third floor apartment inhabited by a guy named Richard. After Aase went to bed, I would just take my cigarette lighter and knock three times on the copper pipe. A couple of minutes later Big John would appear at the door if his wife was asleep.

This usually occurred on Friday and Saturday nights after the girls had gone to bed and we had some energy to spare. We'd open a beer or two and sit for hours playing Atari baseball and football, having a great time. Remember, this was the origins of video gaming, so yes, as it's proven, it's addictive. Some nights, we'd be up to the wee hours of the morning … just one more game, we'd say.

Big John and I became quite proficient at these two Atari games. I don't know if he ever knew I'd marked one of the controllers with an 'X', but I seemed to win most of the baseball and football games and the screen would cheer for every touchdown or home run. Both systems were actually pretty good for 1983/1984 … nothing like today's games, which I can't even figure out.

I still have my Atari unit, all the games and upscale joysticks. I have it in a closet in my study. Big John, who now lives in Nova Scotia wants me to come for a visit and bring my Atari stuff "for old time's sake!"

Sounds like a helluva idea!

POST SCRIPT – *I have invited Big John to write something on these Atari nights in the next chapter.*

Big John is now married to Pyjama Jan, who doesn't seem to mind that he is friends with me, which is nice.

I can be crazy at times, as Pyjama Jan has found out.

~23~ Rod the cod

By Big John

In response to the previous chapter

I don't recall exactly how Rod and I began playing video games but as he has already said, there would be a tap on the heating system to announce a game or two was on. Now, I have never been a 'gamer' either before or after these evenings with Rod. I was more of a table top hockey game kind of guy but upstairs I would go in response to the tap, tap, tap. These games would usually occur after the Saturday night Leaf game on CBC and with no other suitable viewing available and the prospect of free beer, chips and the satisfaction of beating Rod at his own game I was usually more than ready for a little competition with bragging rights on the line.

Once settled in on the left side of his couch, (he had to have the right side, why to this day, I have no idea) the games began. One night as we twisted the controllers in every way imaginable to squeeze some kind of computer game advantage Rod said, "Did you know that I could have played hockey for the Leafs?" "What?" I replied incredulously. "Oh yeah, the Marlies (the Leafs AHL farm team at the time) called and they wanted me to come downtown to the rink for a try out. Man, I could have been playing for the Leafs by now. In fact, you would probably be wearing my sweater and asking for my autograph."

Thinking this was a ruse to get my mind off of the attention level required to defeat whatever impending play he had set for the Atari football game, I asked the obvious. "So ... what happened?" As I eyed his profile from the corner of my eye, seeing him pull on a smoke, swill a mouthful of beer and adjust his oversized paunch.

"Well, I was out at the time and my mother took the call and she didn't tell me for a few weeks and by then it was too late." "That's too bad." I said, and knowing better, I let this tale slide until, glancing out the large window into the frozen night, I replied that we should build a hockey rink out in the backyard and maybe have a skating party or play a little shinny hockey. Rod agreed that this was a great idea and plans for making the rink were set.

On the next available frozen night Rod and I gathered on the only flat part of the backyard and began stomping down the snow to try and compact it. We then began to flood the rink. Hours went by in which we drained the better part of a bottle of liqueur, wondering aloud to each other as to the lack of any significant ice formation except for that which had long ago formed on our eyebrows and day-old whiskers. "Maybe the water is going somewhere." One of us said to the other as we eyed the downhill slope leading to the main street which fronted the property.

Sure enough, as we walked down to street level there was an ice formation across the sidewalk and onto the road that would rival the spectacular frozen ice walls that would appear every winter at Niagara Falls.

"We better shut off the water, turn out the house lights". Rod said. "If someone crashes because of the ice we could be liable, my career as editor of one of Canada's most influential weekly rural newspapers could be jeopardized!" I could feel his paranoia beginning to rise, not really certain if this was the result of one swig too many or a true fear of professional ruin due to a pending litigation.

The sound of an engine approaching from a distance froze us there, fearing that it may be a police patrol on the darkened streets. As we waited and watched, the snow plow drove by, slashing the ice we had created on the road to oblivion and disgorging enough salt to melt most of the Arctic. "Problem solved." I said. " I've gotta crash, see you tomorrow."

The next day we discovered a near perfect ice surface had formed on the rink and donning our skates, sharing the last dregs of the alcohol we joined a few neighbours on the ice. Suffice it to say, after watching Rod skate, the NHL is better off with Rod having pursued a different career.

At this point in writing, my email alert is flashing. It is Rod demanding to know if I would be sending the chapter he requested I write for his new book in time for publication. It was a month or two ago he called and told me he is writing a second book, sent me a chapter he had written about us playing Atari games and asked if I would write the chapter to follow. "Sure" I said. He then went on to tell me that it had to be done in time and it had to be funny. Funny? Funny to me or funny to you or just funny? That is what comedians get paid to do I thought, and just how funny do you think living below you was?

Anyways, I had agreed and now having procrastinated until the last possible day I find myself trying to remember anything funny to write about. The email alert flashed again, it is Rod, increasing my angst. I recall a scene from the movie "Where the Buffalo Roam" starring Bill Murray portraying Hunter S. Thompson. Hunter has committed to a deadline for his publisher, the publisher is harassing Hunter by fax machine much the way that Rod now is harassing me. In reply, Hunter draws a large calibre hand gun from his desk and ends the life of the fax machine.

Now living in Florida, access to large calibre weapons is easy but I know if I do the same to my iPad, my wife will kill me. If fact the iPad is not mine, the computer I am writing on is not mine, I am not sure if I can even save this and email it to Rod or will one wrong key stroke send it into oblivion and I will need to avoid Rod's impending dismay for years to come.

Back upstairs, as the winter progressed, we had played Atari on numerous occasions and both of us were getting quite proficient. It was often by the slimmest of margins that either one of us would win by. It had come to my notice that as Rod was setting up the game, plugging in the controllers that he would always pay close attention to the bottom of each and make a concerted effort to conceal this activity from my view. So on one occasion when Rod left the room to fetch some more beer, I carefully examined the bottom of his controller. Sure enough, a barely visible X had been lightly scratched on the bottom of his. Knowing that to ask him to let me use the "better" controller would be akin to asking a guy to let me use his favourite hockey stick, I devised another plan to equal the playing field. The next night that we played I had a small Phillips screwdriver in my pocket. It was a matter of time before Rod excused himself to the kitchen which allowed me to remove the four screws on the bottom of each controller, exchange the base plate and re-plug the controllers back in so now the X marked the worst controller. To this day, the X still marks the worst controller ... now that is funny.

ROD'S POST SCRIPT – Long John lives outside Halifax now and spends winters in Florida, where he wrote this... completely untouched by myself.

~24~ Let's just 'wing it'

On my 30th birthday, I was still living above Big John and his wife. I was still Editor of The Richmond Hill Liberal. This birthday – a rather important one – The Liberal was holding a massive Golf Tournament for its many advertisers and good clients. I was obligated to attend and play.

This was June 8, 1984. The Tournament was at the luxurious Richmond Hill Golf & Country Club. I was teamed up in a foursome with some advertisers and Kevin McLean, the former Editor of The Liberal and now in Scarborough.

What I was really looking forward to was the big party Aase was throwing me at 70 Main Street, Newmarket when I arrived home. I'd already told my publisher, let's just call him The Drinker, that I'd be leaving right after I finished with golf. More on this later.

As it turned out Kevin McLean and I were tied on the 18th hole and the only thing separating us was the green and our putting. The clubhouse veranda was full as many gathered watched this last group come in. Well, I sunk about a 10-foot putt that had to curve around significantly to the roar of the crowd and the victory over arch-rival Kevin.

I left right after the golf, much to the chagrin of The Drinker Publisher, who was ready to party and wanted me to mingle with the many advertisers on hand. It was a Friday night and I had my birthday party to attend.

I arrived home and had about 30 friends and family stuffed into Aase's apartment and of course Big John and his wife. We had a splendid time partying and eating. After everyone had gone home and Big John's wife at the time, a really 'straight' girl, had gone to bed. Aase, I and Big John were up sitting in the back yard where earlier that winter we had built the skating rink. We were all sitting on some old garden furniture and Aase says about 2 a.m., "I have lots of chicken wings left over." Chicken wings, back then, was a recent phenomenon.

So Aase goes in and heats up the wings and brings out two huge casserole dishes. It's now about 2:30 a.m. and Big John and I are ravenous. We consume the first bunch, which were spicy, but very good. Then Aase says," I tried something special with these, they are 'orange' with real orange peels on them."

Well, if two drunks at 3 a.m. in the morning could eat these 25 to 30 wings any faster, we'd have bones stuck in our throats today – we devoured these special 'orange' chicken wings. They were simply delicious – mouth-watering, in fact. Seriously, we inhaled them.

We complimented Aase over and over and you know what? To this day, Aase has never made them again. She says she lost that special recipe. But for Big John and I at 3 a.m. on my 30th birthday, we were in heaven. To this day, they were the tastiest wings we both ever ate. I talked with Big John last week down in his Florida enclave and he still agreed. An abundance of alcohol and these 'orange' wings were all we needed to cap off my memorable birthday.

It was just a great kick-off to my 30th. It had been extremely hot all day playing golf and as we sat out in mid-20s temperatures, cooling down and eating these scrumptious wings, looking at the stars and talking, I thought "isn't life grand?"

POST SCRIPT – The Drinker Publisher severely reprimanded me early Monday morning when I arrived for work for leaving "without socializing" – meaning drinking with advertisers. I explained it was my 30th birthday and Aase was having a party, but he said "that is no excuse."

The Publisher moved around extensively after his stint at The Liberal. Not because he reprimanded me, but for many other reasons, I wish him a slow, painful death.

Big John, as you know by now eventually married 'Pyjama Jan' and moved to Halifax.

~25~ An unsavoury character

Aase and I have a friend who tends to operate outside of the laws of this land. My good friend Bruce had a poster in his entranceway once that read, "Invite someone dangerous over for tea."

Conrad (not his real name) is that kind of guy. We don't invite him over, he just shows up. Usually when he shows up, he shouldn't be driving. He keeps doing it, despite repeated conversations about drinking and driving. We usually leave his old truck in our driveway and give him a ride back up to his homestead on Lake Simcoe.

One night about six years ago, Aase and I were just sitting in the kitchen talking, when there was a knock at the door. It was this unsavoury Conrad character.

Aase and I were in our pyjamas, so we weren't really expecting company, not to mention a visit from Conrad, who reeked of alcohol.

Conrad sat in the kitchen with us and I offered him a beer, per usual, which he accepted. Shortly after there was a loud rapping at my front door. I wondered 'Who the heck is that? It's about 10:30 on a Tuesday night'?

I open the door to see three York Region Police officers in my little foyer outside of the front door. The one knocking was a female officer, who looked friendly, but by the door was the largest physical specimen I have seen outside of the wrestling arena. Bigger than The Rock of

93

movie fame. My God, he had these huge arms. All three were wearing bullet-proof vests spelling out Police, guns in their holsters. They wanted to see my visitor. Above flew the York Region Police helicopter.

Now, don't get the wrong idea – Aase and I are both law-abiding, solid citizens – we never break the law and certainly live on a quiet street that isn't used to seeing the SWAT team at my front door.

Remember, I'm still in my pyjamas. I fetch Conrad and he talks with the female officer. She said they'd had several motorists phoning in about him and it took a lot of effort to locate him. They chatted about 25 minutes – I was busy holding back my German Shepherd, so I didn't catch it all.

Conrad is quite the storyteller, so I can imagine the bull he fed the officers. His truck was in my driveway. He was in my house. Eventually the officers left with quite the warning, not without scaring the heck out of Aase and me. What the hell is going on?

After they left, we stayed up a while. Aase, being the kind-hearted soul she is, decided it would be better if she drove Conrad home and leave his truck in the driveway, to be picked up at a 'more sober time'.

This all happened about six years ago and Conrad still has quite the laugh that he brought the SWAT team to my little house in Newmarket. All my neighbours, with whom I am good friends, wondered just what was up?

It was a night I'd rather forget!

POSTSCRIPT – Conrad no longer drives so no more worries about him 'dropping in' with who knows what unexpected guests!

~26~ It was Hudak's election to win

As guest columnist Livio Di Matteo correctly pointed out in last Sunday's paper, under the Liberals, Ontario's economy has been in a steady decline, much like Argentina.

I'll go a step further and say our debt-to-resident ratio is higher than in the beleaguered California. Under the Liberals, our provincial debt and deficit have spiraled so that it now sits at $82,000 for a family of four. That's basically $82,000 every family owes the province under the mismanagement by the Liberals.

This was Tim Hudak's election to lose. The man who looks like Michael Keaton pledged to eliminate 100,000 bureaucratic jobs. This was a brain-dead move. Yes, eliminate $4 billion a year from the budget and try to balance the books, but the way he announced it, it had too much shock value.

I don't know how many road signs I saw that declared "Are you willing to risk Hudak?" Yes, the Liberal fear-mongering machine was in full force. With millions spent on television and radio ads, the Liberals, together with all the teachers' unions, OPP union, and God knows what other unions, all decried this pledge from Hudak.

Kathleen Wynne came out so far left, she over-shadowed the NDP's Andrea Horwath. Horwath could only say she'd be more "honest". Even the pollsters - some of them pretty prestigious polling companies - had it all wrong. They were very far off the mark.

In the TV debate, which I watched in its entirety, Hudak came off as a smiling chipmunk, who talked like a smiling chipmunk. Wynne stood her ground, making the promise that the cancellation of the two gas plants would never happen again and Liberals would ensure no more scandals.

Hudak, who also lost to Squinty McGuinty in the 2011 provincial election, could only ensure Ontarians he would create one million jobs. I think Horwath won that debate – no knock-out punches, but she kept up her attack on Wynne. Keep in mind Horwath forced the election by not supporting the Liberal budget, which will now go through in much haste with a majority Liberal government.

After the 2011 debacle which saw Squinty McGuinty returned to power yet again, all the political pundits called on Hudak to be further to the right. Well, he went to the extreme right in this past election and now he'll soon be sent out to pasture.

As Livio Di Matteo said last week, now Ontario's decline is "terminal" under a Liberal government. Letters in The National Post were saying readers are considering moving to Alberta. Ontario is a have-not province and will continue to be a have-not province under the Liberals.

Yes, the urban centres voted Liberal, but our smarter cousins in rural Ontario read the political landscape quite well and voted PC.

Shame on you Ontario.

POSTSCRIPT – The above piece was written to be published in a Metroland newspaper, but alas, it wasn't printed…..a little too strong for the editor to stomach.
However, I fully believe in everything I wrote above.

~27~ The 'burger' affair

So there was a heat wave this past summer. We get a call from Leanie, who is soon to visit her ailing Dad in Markham. Leanie, who lives in Nanaimo with Timmy says she'd like to get a break and come up and visit us in Newmarket.

So, the imaginative guy that I am, I phone Anthony and Katrina, who live in Willow Beach. Anthony grew up with Leanie and hadn't seen her in years. So I arrange for the day that Leanie and her husband Timmy are coming to have Anthony and Katrina come for a visit and a barbe-cue.

The big day comes. Anthony and Katrina are the first to arrive, and soon after Leanie and Timmy show up. It's about 95 degrees Fahrenheit that day, so we put chairs and small tables under our giant maple in the back yard to keep cool.

Well, Leanie is one of two of my wife's oldest friends and they don't see each other that much. So one things leads to another and the beer and liquor start flowing. Yes, we all had designated drivers, with the ex-ception of Aase and I.

We are having a great time sitting in the shade talking about old times, reminiscing and carrying on. I'm just constantly going to the beer fridge for more beer and making drinks. I realize it's getting late. My dear wife Aase is completely gone. She'd been Party Hearty for some time today. She says you'd better get the barbecue on.

Now, folks, my barbecue is not an ordinary barbecue. For one thing, it's charcoal. For another it has a cooking surface that can cook 48 burgers at a time. That statement is from the manufacturer. It's as big as a propane barbecue – a big one. It has a porcelain cooking surface, like the more expensive propane barbecues. It has a smokestack for the smoke. It has levers to raise and lower the charcoal. In a nutshell, this barbecue is a thing of beauty.

Aase is a train wreck by this time and everybody is getting hungry. Thank God Aase has gone shopping and I know where all the food is. So I put on the barbecue, some boneless, skinless chicken breasts – enough for everyone, I put on some small potatoes and carrots in tin foil; I put on enough Italian sausages for everyone, the kind with cheese in the middle. I also put on the barbecue some lobster tails on a stick, still in the shell, but halved.

Remember, it's about 95 degrees. I'm getting hot as hell and operating this thing of beauty barbecue, complete with a heat thermometer that reads 500 degrees F. I'm just dripping with sweat. I mean I'm really boiling over.

Then, I realize, I have to set the outdoor table for everybody. Like I said Aase is a train wreck, so I go in the house and start gathering knives and forks and plates, heat up butter for the lobster, get butter for the potatoes, etc. I start bringing all this stuff out and still keeping an eye on cooking on the barbecue. I ask Timmy to bring out the plates. He does, all six of them, and leaves them in a pile on the table and goes back to the cooling shade under the maple.

So I have to distribute the plates, cutlery, butter, heated butter, etc. Then when everything is just about ready, Leanie comes over to check on me. Try to remember all I'm cooking. Nobody seated under the maple knows what's on the barbecue. Leanie says, "I want a hamburger."

Then she turns around from the barbecue, which is about 20 feet from the maple, and yells, "who wants a burger?" Everyone says yes. Leanie turns to me and exclaims, "That's five burgers, Rod," and marches away.

So now I'm fuming. I'm hot as hell. I have dinner almost ready. They are all still sitting under the maple tree having a good time. Now Leanie wants them all to have burgers. I mean you could fry an egg on my head. I could spit nails.

I go in and prepare the hamburgers, put them on, then the chicken breasts, potatoes, carrots, sausage and lobster are ready. I tell everyone to come and sit down and Timmy is the first. He just grabs a sausage and puts some hot mustard on it and picks it up and starts eating it – he's so hungry. Leanie comes over grabs a lobster tail and before I can inform her how to eat it, she's chomping on the whole thing, shell and all.

Everyone sits down and I serve the chicken breasts to everyone (which I have marinated), put the sausages on the table, distribute the potatoes and carrots and serve the lobster with the melted butter I've prepared. The burgers are still cooking and I'm watching them, while serving everybody.

Well, they all chow down while I'm stuck still cooking these damn five burgers. Leanie has the nerve to say, "I feel bad. You are busy while we are eating." I do a real, real slow burn.

Finally, the burgers are ready, the charcoal is getting pretty low, so they took a long time to cook. Well, by this time, they are all stuffed and hot sitting at the table with no shade. To make me feel better Leanie and Timmy share a burger and Anthony and Katrina share a burger. Yes. That's right, they cut two burgers in half and share half a burger. That's two burgers gone out of five. Meanwhile I've been at the barbecue for a long time and I'm sweating profusely.

My piece of chicken is now cold, the potatoes and carrots are cold.

So I decide to eat one of these famous burgers. While I'm eating, Leanie says "It's too hot here at the table, we're going back under the maple." So I eat two burgers in silence and alone.

Meanwhile, they are carrying on. It's quite the party. I finish up my two burgers and start clearing the table. I get everything in the house and realize I have quite the cleaning job ahead of me. A lot of dishes to be washed, things to be put away, and generally cleaning up.

First thing I do is go into our main floor washroom and stick my head under the tap and run cold water for about five minutes. I really think I was over-heated. I keep my head under the water and then towel myself off.

Then I go out to the kitchen and start this massive clean-up. I work in the house about 20 minutes, then Leanie comes in and exclaims, "Rod, I'm here from Nanaimo and you are ignoring me."

I respond, "As soon as I clean up, I'll be out." I mean there are dishes, cooking utensils and pots everywhere. But inside, I think 'the nerve'!

For weeks after I would loudly yell out to a sober Aase, "Who wants a burger? Five burgers Rod!!!!!" Ticked off is an understatement.

Leanie sent an e-mail a few days later that only said "Thanks for putting up with us."

"Who wants a burger. Five burgers Rod!!!!" I've been uttering that for about six months now. Just for the record, the next morning, Aase asked me, "Did we get dinner?"

Lord, give me strength.

POSTSCRIPT – Leanie went back to her place in Nanaimo with her husband Timmy. I haven't seen her since. She has e-mailed, but I haven't responded. She has corresponded with Aase.

Just a tidbit for my dear readers, at a very young age, Leanie was married to the fellow in Chapter 25 for a very brief time.

Say no more.

~28~ Mystery Monster
In Simcoe depths

FOREWORD – The following appeared in The Era, totally untouched, from the August 8, 1979 edition. Written by myself when I was South Shore Editor of The Era.

LAKE SIMCOE – *"I'm not pulling your leg. I wasn't drunk and I'm not going nuts, but it was there. Believe me!"*

The many fishermen who have had their lines mysteriously snapped by some unknown force and boaters who have spotted a huge creature creeping up from the depths of Lake Simcoe also believe it exists. They have labeled it Kempenfelt Kelly or the Loch Simcoe Monster.

Huron Indian folklore describes it as a massive, long-necked serpent which surfaces on eerie, moonlit nights. They call it Igopogo.

Whatever name you give this mysterious degenerate from the prehistoric era, it was sighted again just last week.

Last year The Era received a report that a strange creature was seen off Willow Beach. The three local residents involved did not want their names used, so the story was dropped.

However, a week ago, a Snake Island cottager, fishing not far from shore, felt something brush underneath of his small craft and then it partially surfaced approximately 10 feet away.

"It was the ugliest thing I have ever seen," he exclaimed in an interview last week.

This witness, too, did not want his name used. He is a businessman and feared losing his professional credibility.

Mr. Quint, not his real name, told The Era that the monster from the watery depths of Lake Simcoe was approximately 20 to 30 feet in length, with an unattractive head of a boxer dog.

Mr. Quint also noted that it had a sporadic array of flippers or fins along its body.

"It looked like three trout mated together with a boxer dog," he continued, trying to explain its appearance. "It just didn't look like anything I've ever seen before … it was pretty scary."

WILLOW BEACH SIGHTING

The comment which opens this report was made last week by one of three woman who spotted the creature moving in towards shore as they were driving along Lake Drive at Willow Beach one year ago.

Mrs. Black (not her real name) stated, "I've never seen anything like it, before or after."

Sometime last August, she stated, the trio were driving past the beach when one of them spotted a "big hump in the water," moving in to shore.

'MY GOD, WHAT IS THAT?"

Her companion, Mrs. Shultz (not her real name), remembered saying to herself, "My God, what is that? … All I could think of was that there is no bloody rock that big out there that big …You just couldn't take your eyes off it."

She said that the monster was about 100 yards off shore, when they first spotted it. Then it came into shore and "scared the hell out of us."

"It looked like a big rock (the hump) and about 10 feet from that was another sort of little rock. They both looked like they had been in the water for a long time and turned brown," she continued.

"We just sat there and watched it submerge and the water rippled around it and then it started towards shore. The water rippled in big circles and it came in to about 25 feet. It made an abrupt turn and headed right back out into the lake and we watched it as far as we could see."

"When it went out, there were foot-high waves coming in on the beach, but if you looked further down the beach there weren't any waves," she remarked.

Mrs. Shultz also stated that there was a young girl in a canoe with a friend on the shore at the time. The creature came very close to her, she said, and "She was mesmerized. After it went back out into open water, they just pulled the canoe out of the water and left."

Mrs. Shultz noted it was about 6:30 p.m. and the water was "like glass" when their sighting of the monster took place. The next night she heard a news report about a Barrie woman who said she had spotted such a creature approximately one hour later the day before while sailing on the other side of the lake.

"I know the area and when that came on it really scared me. Whatever it was, it wasn't small," she said.

She and her two friends decided to tell the press their story but only if they could remain anonymous.

This is the first time their story has been printed.

This is a pencil drawing of an artist's rendition of the Loch Simcoe Monster.

Artwork by Sam Logan

BEST ACCOUNT

The best account of a sighting of the Loch Simcoe Monster was by a minister and a funeral director and their families while boating in Cook's Bay in 1963.

Rev. Bill Williams, formerly of Mount Albert (he has since moved to Winnipeg) and his wife and two children joined Neil and Marjory Lathangue of Bradford and their child for a leisurely day of boating on the Lathangues' cabin cruiser.

Mr. Lathangue said in an interview last week that the incident occurred around 7 p.m. when the water was "just like a mirror."

"I was operating the boat and sitting up higher than everybody else," he recalled. "I guess they were talking to me and as it came up alongside of us, I turned my head and they also turned around and I remember the Reverend's first words, 'Great Scot, it's a lake monster'!"

He estimated its length between 30 and 70 feet, comparing it to their 26-foot cruiser.

"He was just travelling at the water line and he had a blunt head which the water was just rolling over," Mr. Lathangue explained. "(From the head) it went back about six or seven feet and then there were four dorsal fins out of the water about 10 inches, charcoal and scaly looking. Then it went back another eight feet and there was another identical set of dorsal fins," he stated.

"I'm convinced it's a lake monster or whatever you want to call it," he remarked. "We got a pretty good look at it."

The group decided not to say anything about the incident because they feared people would think they were a little "crazy," but the word got around and the Reverend gave his report on a Barrie radio station a day later.

Mrs. Lathangue also said last week, "It wasn't a dream or our imagination, there is definitely something in that lake, there just has to be."

The Lathangue incident has since been reported in a book entitled, In Search of Lake Monster, (Peter Costello, $1.75, distributed by Coles Bookstore Ltd.).

Ron Desjardins, a fisheries biologist with the Ministry of Natural Resources' Lake Simcoe Fisheries Assessment Unit, stationed at Sibbald Point Provincial Park said in a recent interview he did not believe it was a lake monster these eyewitnesses saw.

"In my estimation, it is probably a big fish – what kind of fish I don't know."

"There are some very, very large lake trout in there. We've seen fish as large as 37 lbs.," he noted. "Northern Pike can get in the range of the high 20 and 30 lbs. ... Muskie can be very big, and channel catfish are very large, so you know people could see quite a large fish moving in the water and not exactly perceive what it is," he explained.

"It may look to be something quite strange. Sometimes people aren't familiar with fish that grow that large," he added.

Mr. Desjardins said such a sighting could actually be a sturgeon, but pointed out that they haven't been spotted in Lake Simcoe since 1956.

"They are rarely seen, however, and can grow quite large," he stated.

"The Assessment Unit, he continued, estimated there are some 40,000 fishermen on the lake over the summer months and 100,000 in the winter."

"I think it has been estimated that Lake Simcoe supplies 15 per cent of the angling in Ontario," he noted.

Of that number, the unit's staff talks to approximately 8,000 fishermen each year and stories of a monster "generally don't come up," he said.

"I guess they are embarrassed about it. We just don't hear much about it at all," he added.

COULD BE LAKE TROUT

Stories concerning fishermen's lines pulled through the ice hole in the winter, he said, "could easily be a large lake trout."

As for large ripples spotted on the water's surface in the summertime, he maintains that northern pike cruise very close to the surface and "create quite a ripple effect."

He did admit, however, that sightings do occur and "whatever it may be, I don't know, I tend to think in terms of it being a fish that we know are in the lake."

Similar to the Loch Ness Monster or Nessie, as she's been labeled, we'll just never know the mystery of the Loch Simcoe Monster until either remains are found or it decides to get friendly with a fishery biologist.

POSTSCRIPT – As mentioned, I wrote this in 1979, during the summer.

This story actually created a frenzy as many youngsters refused to go into the water again for fear of the monster.

This story was written a few years after the original Jaws movie came out, which in itself, created quite the fear of sharks.

~29~ Do the murky waters hide a monster?

FOREWORD – The following was written by myself and run in the Newmarket-Aurora Era-Banner on Nov. 11, 1990.

*Sightings of the Lake Simcoe Monster, Kempenfelt Kelly, have been reported in the past 90 years by youthful fishermen, a minister and a funeral director. Are the stories true?

Do monsters really exist?

That question has plagued the minds of men for centuries.

Futile attempts have been made by a number of nations to locate the evasive Loch Ness Monster, to no avail.

Sonars, high tech submarines and submersible microphones have been used, but there is no concrete evidence that the Loch Ness Monster or Messiteras Rhombptteryx exists.

Like sightings of Nessie, as she is affectionately known, there is a bevy of information in historical data of sightings of the Loch Simcoe Monster.

It is estimated to be anywhere from 30 to 50 feet in length and have the unattractive head of a boxer dog.

In the Barrie Examiner, Centennial edition, in 1953, it headlined a story, "What happened to the sea serpent of Lake Simcoe?"

As it recalled, "local citizens were inclined to scoff at the idea of such a leviathan in the water of the lake … and great arguments were carried on throughout the town as to whether such a creature existed, but it was actually reported sighted at the beginning of May, 1900."

"A group of young boys decided that they would spend the evening fishing, so they went down to the wharf at the foot of Mulcaster Street one Tuesday night. They were actively engaged in their sport when one of the youngsters let out a scream, at the same time pointing out over the water."

"A large, dark object was seen approaching the wharf and as it came in, lifted itself partly out of the water. This was too much for the youngsters. They dropped their fishing rods and bolted as fast as they could."

However, as fate would have it, their shouts were heard by some passersby, who went down to see what was happening.

One man described what he saw in the following way: "The monster lifted from the water a head like that of a horse and flapped the surface from time to time with its huge fan-like tail."

Some of the stout-hearted citizens who went down to watch this phenomenon actually threw stones at the serpent, but, as reports tell, "these did not seem to disturb it in the least, for it took its own time to finally sink beneath the surface and disappear in the bay."

And then, there's the story from the Northern Advance, of May 1903. "A couple of badly scared Grand Trunk detectives landed at Carley's boathouse on Tuesday claiming that Barrie's famous sea serpent had suddenly appeared out in the bay within a few rods of their boat. The agitation of the men was such that there is no doubt they saw something. But the statement that it had a head as big as a dog's and had horns will have to be taken with a grain of salt.

It is thought that one of Cliff Carley's muskrats bobbed up suddenly near the boat and as suddenly went down again, giving the detectives hardly enough time to form an idea as to the appearance of the monster of the deep."

And from a Fred Grant scrapbook, came this article from the Barrie Examiner of 1950: "David Soules recalled some experience which he and a brother had with a sea serpent. There used to be a sea serpent which spent much of its time in the water and on the shore near here. It was up around Orillia at times too, because we would hear frequent reports that someone had seen it. The first time ever I saw it was years ago. My brother and I were washing sheep down at the shore. We heard a loud splash in the water and a short way out we saw a huge long thing go through the water like a streak. It went around a little point and we followed it."

"Apparently, it had gone into the swamp around the point and we followed it. When we got there, we found a deep wide trail in the mud."

He described it as having fin-like appendages and being very large and very ugly looking.

"It was as long as from here to the other side of the road," said Soules, indicating a distance of about 35 feet.

And people also have fun with the monster theory. When The Era ran a story on the Loch Simcoe Monster in its August 8, 1979 edition, Sutton businessman Rolf Engler picked up on the idea and approached town council.

Engler told a township industry and tourism committee he planned to market T-shirts, hot plates and other items with a drawing of Igopogo on them along with a map of Lake Simcoe, with towns around the lake marked.

Engler suggested the township use the same theme of Igopogo's existence for signs at Georgina's borders saying, "Welcome to the home of Igopogo."

Industry and tourism committee chairman John McLean said the design was "cute."

The committee deferred any recommendations about the Igopogo theme and has yet to pick up on the idea.

However, Barrie did. According to the Toronto Star of March 13, 1985, "The Lake Simcoe beastie has been named the official mascot of Kempenfelt, a holiday weekend that winds up tomorrow."

Festival T-shirts and posters were designed depicting Kelly as a "sort of dumb dinosaur, wagging its tail above the waterline. He has a goofy grin and goo-goo eyes."

However, in the same Star story, it related the tale of two Toronto fishermen who said they saw the monster while fishing on Cook's Bay.

"It was over 15 feet long and must have weighed close to 1,000 pounds," said Jean-Claude Bergeron of Logan Ave. He said he and his companions feared they would be devoured by a beast with a "camel's hump and a tail about seven feet long."

Andreas Trottman wants to hear from you if you've seen something.

As a member of the International Society of Cryptozoology, the science of unknown or mysterious animal structure, Trottman is part of an organization which has researched Scotland's Loch Ness Monster.

According to the Barrie Examiner of Nov. 11, 1989, Trottman, wants to know what residents here have seen in Lake Simcoe.

"Loch Ness is not the only lake with sightings, only the most famous," said Trottman, who's been involved in this sort of thing for about 17 years.

Trottman makes it clear he's not searching for sea monsters or anything prehistoric in the chilly waters of Lake Simcoe and Kempenfelt Bay, but something just a little more believable.

"It could be a big fish or it could be a metamorphosis of a different kind of animal," Trottman said, while noting he wants to look at the situation with "both feet on the ground."

"On the other hand, the mysterious side of the whole situation is very interesting," he added.

What makes sense to Trottman and his society is that some form of fish or reptile or mammal – or something evolved from them – could have ended up in Lake Simcoe.

It might have come from the ocean, down the St. Lawrence and eventually made its way to the Great Lakes and some of its rivers and tributaries.

Do monsters really exist? And, more specifically in Lake Simcoe? We don't know for sure, but it's certainly food for thought, isn't it?

POSTSCRIPT – As I said off the top, this story ran in The Era-Banner Nov. 11, 1990.

I took out some of the paragraphs you had already read in the previous chapter.

~30~ My Hunter night

FOREWORD – My very good friend, Susie Kockerscheidt, current photographer for York Region Media Group, said the following chapter should be included in my new book. I agreed with Susie, who I originally gave a start in photography when I was Editor of the Georgina Era-Banner, back in the late 1980s and early 1990s.

In my 40-something years in newspapers, I had many, many Hunter S. Thompson-type escapades. For those of you who don't know of Hunter S. Thompson, he was the predominant journalist of his time. He invented Gonzo Journalism and wrote many memorable articles for Rolling Stone magazine. He led a drug-induced frenzy of a life, until actor Johnny Depp finally blew his ashes out of a cannon on Hunter's property in Aspen.

But I'm getting off track. Back when I left the Richmond Hill Liberal, it would be about 1986, I was hired by Editor John Slykhuis of the Independent News. Now the Independent News was started by a group of newspaper people who had worked at Topic and had seen the writing on the wall.

Back then you could start a newspaper. There were no iPhones, no computers, no internet. People got their written information from newspapers. The cream of the crop was that infamous newspaper, The Topic, whose staff decided to create their own paper to cover Newmarket called – The Independent News.

Now, let me take a minute to talk about The Topic. It was a revolutionary newsmagazine – way ahead of its time. I would have loved to have worked on it. It was mainly spearheaded by John Slykhuis, although Marney Beck was Editor for a while. At one point, it circulated in all of York Region and was the closest thing to a regional paper this region has ever seen and will ever see.

I highly respected John and I'd known him for a few years when he hired me at The Independent News as Sports Editor – but he knew I was capable of much more. That was the only job opening.

I can't exactly remember the year, but there was a municipal election in Newmarket. Mayor Ray Twinney was up against Bud Walford, a councilor, for the mayor's seat. Everything else was meaningless in that election. This was a battle royal. (I could write a book about my relationship with the late Ray Twinney, who called me 'Ron' for 30 years. How about the time he chased me around town for a week because I called him The Godfather of Sports in Newmarket, right after The Godfather movie came out in theatres. Man was he pissed at me).

Anyway, I detract. So election night, John Slykhuis asks me to take photos of the mayor's race and work alongside him. He'd take the notes, I'd take the photos and add some colour. This was going to be quite the mayor's race.

So in Hunter S. Thompson fashion, right after work, we head to the local watering hole – Fitzy's. We both smoked and back then you could smoke in bars, so we sat around smoking and we consumed about six beers each till the polls closed and results were starting to come in.

We get in John's old jalopy (newspaper people back then only drove old rickety cars) and we head to the campaign headquarters of Ray Twinney, which was in his basement. It was absolutely jammed with supporters and included an open bar and piles of food.

After John and I consume way more beers, it's obvious Twinney will retain his mayor's seat. John does his interview, I take some photos and we head back to the offices of The Independent News. It was about 1 a.m. and the paper would leave at 3 a.m. to be on the streets early the next morning. And we were both hammered.

We get back to the office. Now Mike Barrett was the head photographer and I don't know how to process film. Yes, I was using film back then. So either Mike or his helper processes my film, John starts writing his story, with myself adding colour here and there. While we are waiting for the film PMT (Photo Mechanical Transfer), John says, "You'd better phone Bud Walford for a comment or two."

So at 2 a.m. I phone Bud Walford's campaign headquarters. I get somebody, I don't know who, on the phone, explain who I am and then I wait for a good 15 minutes for Bud to come on the phone. I start asking my questions and taking notes, but it's obvious, like me, he'd had a lot to drink and his language is – let's say – colourful.

I get a quote from Bud, it goes in the story and then we have to run the story off on those old Kaypro machines, paste it up with knife and wax, along with my photos, and voila the paper is ready for press.

John and I get all that done, assemble the whole newspaper, which had already been mostly done, place it in the printing box and the driver comes in to take it to Hamilton to be printed.

It was really a memorable edition the next day – colourful election story on Twinney winning and I took a good shot of Twinney with his supporters whooping it up. And yes, we also had all the other election results in that paper.

Needless to say, John and I slept in the next day. My Hunter S. Thompson election night coverage with my old buddy John – a memorable affair. Like many ink-stained wretches before us, when we were done, it was quite late, we were drunk, and we had put a paper to bed.

POSTSCRIPT – Mayor Ray Twinney died of cancer many years ago. He took a train trip across Canada with his beloved wife just before he died and I was among many at the Newmarket train station waving and wishing him well.

John Slykhuis is retired, writes the odd piece in The Georgina Advocate, and lives near Sibbald Point Provincial Park.

Photog Mike Barrett still works for York Region Media Group.

~31~ This 'spin-doctoring' makes my blood boil

FOREWORD – The following column appeared in the Summer 2012 issue of Horse Talk. It was also picked up by the Canadian Thoroughbred Society for their national website and received many, all-favourable comments.

I really get quite infuriated when Toronto newspapers and even my local community paper try to cover what the Liberal government is doing to the horse racing industry.

In my local newspaper this morning, they referred to the revenue-sharing agreement that has been in place between the Liberal government and the horse racing industry for more than 10 years as a "subsidy."

Only a writer completely inexperienced or completely lacking in knowledge about the horse racing industry would refer to this as a "subsidy." It really makes my blood boil to see inexperienced, young, naïve writers buy "into" donut-eating Finance Minister Dwight Duncan's complete "spin-doctoring" and "propaganda" on this issue.

It was the rather flabby Duncan who first called this revenue-sharing agreement – an agreement that was negotiated in good faith – a "subsidy." Nothing could be further from the truth.

The bottom line, cancellation of this agreement will immediately see the loss of 60,000 directly-related jobs and literally thousands of spin-off and secondary jobs, not to mention the decimation of the horse racing stables and the whole horse racing industry in general.

These so-called journalists even buy into the propaganda that there will be extra money by killing the slots at the track program and this "extra" money will go into health care and education and "benefit all Ontarians."

What complete hogwash. The Ontario Lottery and Gaming Corporation (OLG) has plans to build mega-casinos. Maybe kill the smaller casinos and get everybody into gambling, which this Liberal government considers "easy money."

The billions this minority Liberal government made off the revenue-sharing agreement with the horse racing industry now has to be replaced. There is no extra money for health care and education – what a complete fallacy.

In my opinion, this dastardly Liberal government, led by Squinty McGuinty, just wants us all to become complete gambling addicts. Is this the direction you want this province to head in? I certainly don't.

Small wagering on horse racing is more like a minor-league hobby, than die-hard gambling addicts, who go into massive debt to cover their addictions. Betting on the ponies, in my mind, is not part of that action at all. In the words of Uncle Buck (John Candy) you are going for the excitement – the colourful jockeys and beautiful horses – you are not sitting at some machine, mindlessly pulling on a lever.

Race tracks provided the building, put in the slots, and the province racked in the money, giving the horse racing industry a "small cut." Now they've announced they will cut it in 2013.

Oh, yes, the Liberals have pledged $50 million to help smooth over the transition to the horse racing industry, even set up a panel of three former ministers. Big hairy deal. I predict the horse racing industry in

Ontario will just dry up.

Last night, I was at a stable that was breeding race horses. They are now winding down the operation – getting out of the business completely. Toronto papers have also been reporting on alleged euthanizing of new foals so they don't have to pay the stud fee and also the year-long cost of raising the foal.

No, this Liberal government is just an unfeeling, tax-creating, money-grubbing, spin-doctoring group of total programmed politicians. Do I sound angry? You bet I am.

Just as an example, now the Liberals are considering making bicycle helmets mandatory for adults. They already are for children, but the Chief Coroner in Ontario is recommending these helmets for adults – what complete hogwash.

It's just another, pure example of how we are over-governed in Ontario and how this Liberal government is an aimless boat afloat in a sea of debt – debt created by old Squinty McGuinty and his misguided policies.

I was going to write about 'I'll Have Another', and how we could have had the first triple crown winner wince 1978, but when I received my local paper this morning I realized the 'true' message of what this Liberal government has planned for Ontario has to come out, without all the massaging of the message.

NEWS FLASH – After writing this column, I heard a radio report that this will be the final Queen's Plate at Woodbine because of the McGuinty cuts and Woodbine will eventually shut down….after more than 100 years of the running of the Queen's Plate!

Rod Urquhart is Contributing Editor of Horse Talk and can be reached at: roderick.urquhart@gmail.com.

POST SCRIPT – As it turned out, it was not the last Queen's Plate.

Much has been written about Squinty and donut-eating Duncan in the three years after.

As I predicted in the column above, the horse racing industry was decimated and is only now starting to get back on 'track' (excuse the pun).

After the funds were cut by Duncan, many racetracks shut down forever and many, many jobs were lost and foals euthanized.

That is the legacy of Squinty McGuinty, the worst Premier this province has ever seen.

~32~ Tahiti Treat water skiing

You know, years ago, before I met my wife, I lived with a girl named Shelley. My wife now calls her "Smelly Shelley."

We were good friends with Misener before he met his wife. Misener, as mentioned, had a cottage up in Sundridge, owned by his parents.

His Dad asked the three of us to go up, spend a week, and paint the board and batten cottage. It was your typical one floor, three bedroom, living room, bathroom, kitchen cottage, on a nice lot right by the water with the train tracks behind. In fact, when the trains went by the lamps and pictures would shake on the walls – that's how close the tracks were. His Dad had some really early Playboy magazines, which I loved to look through. No, I'm not a perv, these magazines back then devoted a lot of space to really quality writers. They were great reading. The photos of girls were actually funny. He had one magazine that featured Marilyn Monroe in a bikini.

So up we went to paint the cottage. It was always painted dark brown. We all had the week off from our new jobs. We had just finished university. Well, we had that cottage all painted in two and a half days, then it was time to Party On Dude!

After lunch one day, a bit later, Smelly and Misener got into the vodka. Now, this was a cottage with limited resources on hand, but

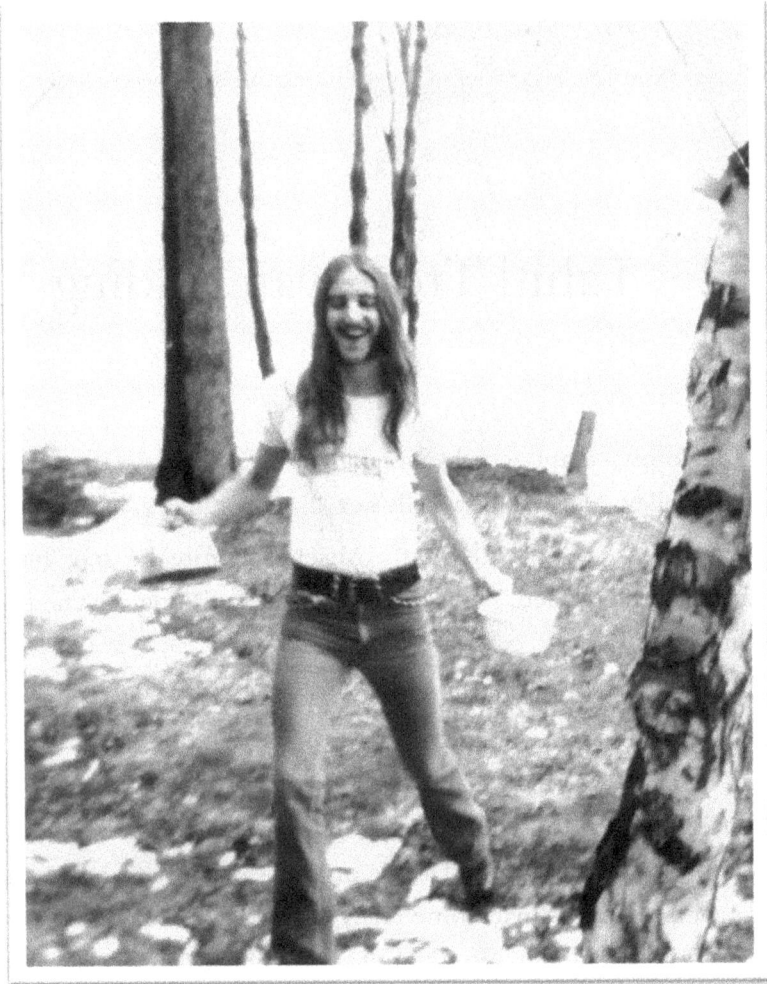

The Misener gets some water from the lake during
the famous Tahiti Treat weekend.
Photo by Rod Urquhart

there seemed to be an unlimited supply of the pop Tahiti Treat. So it
doesn't need to be said that they soon were mixing up vodka with Tahiti Treat – a red sugary drink.

I decided I wanted to go water skiing. I really hadn't started the libations yet. So Smelly and Misener get some pre-mixed vodka and Tahiti Treat in a thermos and plastic glasses and we head out in the boat.

Soon I get up on two skis, then drop one. Everything is going along fine. Misener and Smelly are really enjoying their drinks. Then, without them paying attention we head near shore. I look down and it's so shallow, the boat's motor is stirring up the bottom. It's about two feet of water. I think if I wipe out, I'm going to be a goner.

So I start screaming, "Shallow water!" Well, Misener isn't even looking ahead. Smelly and him are severely enjoying this new mixed cocktail. I yell again, "Shallow water!" I hear Smelly shout, "He wants to go faster!"

So Misener speeds up the boat. But finally, thank God, realizes that he's in quite shallow water and headed into even shallower water, and he finally heads back out into the deeper waters of Lake Bernard, which is a massive island-free lake, just north of Huntsville.

I had to stay on my ski until we returned to shore, because by this time they were polluted and I doubted they'd be able to pick me up if I dunked it. Both were soon sleeping it off once we settled back into the cottage. That's my Tahiti Treat Ski Story!

POST SCRIPT – Misener's father died as mentioned earlier, but his mom was still alive at the time of writing and still goes up to the family cottage in Sundridge each summer, with Misener driving her up.

I really have found memories of this cottage and Misener's parents, who treated me like their own.

~33~ Who wants pizza?

You know sometimes in the newspaper business you get severely stabbed in the back. That's the case of 'The Snide.'

I hired The Snide three times, the first time at the Metro North News as Sports Editor, the second time as a reporter when I switched over to The Newmarket Era and a third time when I was Editor of the Georgina Era-Banner. I hired him as a freelance reporter, and he ended up stabbing me in the back.

After working for Metroland for years, I went with Citizens Communications Group, better known as CCG. I was editor of a number of publications, including York Business News magazine, Voice of the Farmer and Spotlight entertainment news publications. But, if that wasn't enough, I filled in once a week typing in copy at The Georgina Advocate with my friends John Slykhuis and Susie Kockerscheidt.

John was editor and Susie was photographer and I was a typesetter. I type incredibly fast. John used to let me write columns and I would write one about once a month. The Town of Georgina was introducing buck-a-bag garbage collection, with the suggestion of $2 a bag. Now nowhere else in York Region do they pay for their garbage to be picked up. As far as I know everybody gets a limit, and can put garbage out for free, but this was revolutionary in Georgina. It raised the ire of many residents. One councillor did not get re-elected for suggesting $2 a bag.

The Snide, who was with The Georgina Era-Banner, wrote a column saying there were 100 people at the council meeting to discuss this. After this, I wrote a column in The Advocate questioning this statistic as I had heard that the council chambers were jammed top and bottom, the halls were jammed and the front entrance was jammed. Speakers for the council meeting had to be set up outside the council chambers. I heard it was simply overflowing. The Snide set the number at 100. He didn't say approximately. I said in The Advocate, there had to be more than 100 residents in attendance to voice their displeasure with paying a buck-a-bag.

Well, the night The Advocate with my column came out, I took my wife out for a birthday dinner to the House of York. Anybody who is anybody, knows of the House of York if they lived in northern York Region. We had a wonderful steak and lobster dinner.

We came home to our house and then all hell started breaking loose. As soon as we got home, the phone rang. I answered and the person hung up. About 15 minutes later, the pizzas started arriving – one after the other – about 15 in all – over a 35 minute span. It got so bad, two or three pizza drivers would see other pizza drivers in the driveway and not even bother coming to our door. They could realize what was going on – it was a nasty practical joke.

Aase had no idea of what was going on. They had our name, address and phone number. Aase paid for the first two, then I put a stop to it. I knew what was going on. This was The Snide's way of getting back at me. He and I had been friends and he told me once of a teacher that pissed him off, so he sent 20 pizzas to his house.

Pizzas kept arriving at the door. Each box I would phone and see if they had a number on record of who ordered the pizzas. I said I was going to call the police. Not one of these 14 to 16 pizza companies had a record of who had called and couldn't even recall the conversation. Pizza Pizza said they had just dropped recording the numbers (this was before call display).

The Snide went away unchallenged. I didn't retaliate. I didn't even call him. I wasn't going to stoop to his level. Soon after he was out of a job, but it certainly wasn't my doing. It was restructuring.

And you know also how I know it was him? Because he dropped off the minutes of that particular council meeting with the Town Clerk's report that said "about 100 residents were on hand" circled in yellow and a note to show Rod on my wife's desk at The Era-Banner. She brought it home and showed me. I knew instantly.

What hurts most was The Snide and I once were great friends. It was a nasty thing to do on Aase's birthday and after a great dinner. I know you have to forgive and forget, but I wish The Snide a slow and painful death. He's really a sick individual if you get to know him. Maybe that's why Aase never liked him.

POSTSCRIPT – Last I heard The Snide had taken a job in Timmins. Then I heard he was out near Windsor. Whatever, I don't need to keep in touch with that idiot.

He always lived paycheck to paycheck, living in basement apartments and driving some old wreck.

Good riddance.

John Slykhuis, who edited this book, wrote me that "closer to 200 to 250 people were at that meeting.

I was at that meeting," reported John.

~ 34 Do frogs exist? ~

Many years ago, prior to going back to The Era-Banner, I worked for a paper called the Metro North News. That paper evolved from The Independent News, mentioned in chapter 33. The Metro North News was owned in part by a guy named Chuck Connors. He sold interests in the Newmarket publication to Dennis Mills, an MP. Later it was taken over by Magna founder Frank Stronach, then returned to Chuck Connors until his early, untimely death. It survived a few months after that, then disappeared.

But, in its heyday, it was quite a newspaper. It came out weekly, on Wednesdays, and was usually about 60 pages. A tabloid, it was well-respected and The Era-Banner people sure took notice, hiring quite a few of us away to Metroland, like myself.

Big John Slykhuis was editor and he hired me as reporter. I was more than reporter, however, given the responsibility of proofing the paper each week and pasting up most of it. (Back then the copy came out in long strips, you had to cut it, then put hot wax on the back and stick it to the pages. Very time consuming and not at all like the pagi-nation today using a Mac).

One night, not long after I was working there, John Slykhuis asked me to proof his column closely. I did and changed his use of "Frog" in referring to Quebecers. (Remember this was many years ago and

Quebec was making all kinds of demands or saying they'd separate). I took all the "Frogs" in reference to Quebecers out of John's column, paginated the rest of the paper. Made sure it was ready to go to the printer, and I went home. About 3 a.m.

Well, Big John, after I left, pulled out my edited copy waxed down and put in his original column. (Those who remember the early days of The Bradford Witness and The Topic will recall John's fiery, scathing columns. This is what ran in The Metro North News, this time attacking Quebecers).

Big John got a call from Dennis Mills who was quite upset with this column. That's really an understatement. So Big John tells Chairman Mills the 'what for' and the next thing I know I'm driving Big John home to Bradford because he no longer has a company car and was just fired.

Now this really upset me. Here was my good friend out of a job, a job he'd had for years after leaving The Topic. But you got to admire him – he is opinionated and he stuck with his column. He wouldn't run a retraction, as requested by Chairman Mills.

Gotta admire that in a man.

But Big John had a wife and two children. Not the greatest of scenarios.

What happened next was mind-numbing to myself. A few days later, after the dust had settled, I talked to Chuck Connors about becoming Editor. Instead he appointed a non-talent guy. This non-talent guy just played video games in his office all day and I did all the Editor's work, minus the pay. In fact this non-talent guy hardly wrote a thing. I did all the editing and pagination. It wasn't long before Frank Stronach bought the paper. They offered me a $5,000 bonus if I stayed, but I took a job as Editor of the Georgina Era-Banner. I'd had enough of the bull dung.

POST SCRIPT – I see John Slykhuis about once a week and we remain good friends.

In fact, he edited this book.

John writes very little these days, the odd column in The Era *or* Advocate, *and makes his home in Sutton.*

His wife died a few years ago and his children are all grown up and making their own way in the world.

~35~ Lord of the flies

After John Slykhuis was fired, and Non-Talent took over as editor, I was made News Editor. Believe me I did all the work of an editor and other managers approached me when they needed the editor.

One such manager was The Cute One (I'm not gay, but that's what all the girls said). He was Advertising Manager. He had an office right next to mine. We became great friends. He really didn't like Non-Talent, although he had worked with him before. The Cute One really generated a lot of sales at Metro North News, motivating a large sales staff, and later took a job with Metroland. He's still with Metroland and has had quite the successful career, becoming a General Manager.

I had one those little children's basketball nets and little ball, that some managers like The Cute One would come into my office to talk to me and we'd have a quick game of basketball up to 10 baskets. We'd socialize together and I'd often go down to his apartment in Aurora, have a few brown pops and hang out. He had a great stereo system.

As mentioned in the previous chapter, we had to use this wax machine, that heated up paraffin wax to coat the backs of the strips of copy. Then they were cut with an X-acto blade and placed on the flats (pages). Photos had to be done this way also, but they were PMT's – Photo Mechanical Transfers.

One Christmas, my sister Tracy gave me a bag of 250 real-life looking black house flies. I knew exactly what to do with them. The Cute One was meticulous – he always kept his office quite clean. If the sign of a sick mind is a clean desk, The Cute One never bought into that saying.

I used to work quite late Sunday and Monday nights, until about 4 a.m. getting ready for the Wednesday paper delivery. So after everybody went home one Sunday night, I took out this package of flies and with a credit card, opened The Cute One's office door. Very slowly (and this took a long time) I waxed all four feet of these real-life looking house flies and walked from the composing room next door to his office and I placed these 250 flies everywhere I could in his office.

Altogether, it took about three hours to finish the job. I usually worked, like I said until 4 a.m., but this night I went home at 7 a.m., just prior to The Cute One arriving for work.

Well. I had waxed flies stuck all over his desk, all over his telephone, notebooks, wall, wall art, the back of the door – basically everywhere you looked, there were these flies. His office really looked like an infestation of flies had struck during the night. I thought it was a thing of beauty. You see with this paraffin hot wax on their feet, these plastic flies could stick on anything.

Well, I was home sleeping when he came in, but I heard he wasn't too pleased, asking where "all these damn flies came from?" Like I said, his office was covered in them. When I heard of his response, I laughed and laughed – mission accomplished.

A lot of these newspaper chapters in this book would get anyone fired today. Imagine if someone decorated his office today with plastic flies? They'd be shown the door. But back before times were politically correct and people didn't take life so seriously, we had a lot of fun … something that I think is missing from today's newsrooms.

POSTSCRIPT – The Cute One recently started coming back to York Region after working up north for years. He now covers both areas and is still a widely-respected Metroland General Manager.

I'm pretty sure he was scooped up from The Metro North News prior to Frank Stronach having any interest in the newspaper.

~36~ They stole our Dick – Her Majesty was not amused

After John Slykhuis was fired from The Metro North News (see chapter 34), our renowned freelancer for that paper, Dick Illingworth, decided he was going to have a party in John's honour, with just a few of us guys who worked with him.

Now, I could write an entire book about Dick and I sincerely hope somebody does someday. In later years, Dick was the supreme freelancer for newspapers. At the same time as writing for The Metro North News, he wrote for Metroland and had a rant on Rogers cable almost every night. Dick was everywhere and writing about it – and he was approaching 80 years of age.

Dick led a distinguished career. He was an RCAF navigator in World War Two, he worked at Queen's Park for years as the air force attaché to four Lieutenant Governor's. He served as Mayor of Aurora for two terms. His first wife had died at the time of John's party, but years later he married celebrated artist Dorothy Clark McClure. To me Dick was an 'icon'.

John had given him his first job as a freelancer and Dick never forgot that. Dick never forgot a lot of things. His main interest was theatre and the arts, maybe how he met Dorothy, and he wrote terrific theatre reviews. I really can't say enough about Dick. He was everywhere and on top of everything.

After John was let go and Non-Talent was made Editor of The Metro North News, he didn't run much of Dick's stuff. In fact, many on-going plays, crying for publicity, for which Dick wrote the reviews, didn't run – even though the Metro North News was always over 60 pages of tabloid news.

I'll never forget the day Dick came into the Metro News offices and let Non-Talent have it – full barrels. As Dick stormed out, he said "I quit. I'm dedicating my writing to Metroland and The Banner and The Era." I was in the Composing Room when all this went down. I wrote the headline in The Metro North News the next week, "The Banner stole our Dick," and I wrote a tribute to Dick Illingworth. This was obviously prior to the party for John. However, I ramble.

So the night came for the party for John. It was a very cold blustery night. Dick had made a big pot of chili for us. He drank wine but had lots of beer on hand for the four of us gathered. Despite being Mayor of Aurora and all he had done, Dick had a modest house in Aurora. We retired to his recreation room in the basement. This room was filled with photos and letters and memorabilia of Dick's earlier life. I read most of it and Dick had led an astonishing life – and this was before his long freelance career.

So we eat our chili and Dick lights a fire in his small wood-burning fireplace. We consumed multiple beers and ate bowls of his delicious chili. Dick enjoyed his wine, and he certainly enjoyed it that night, throwing log after log on the fire, amid a shower of sparks, which I stamped out.

He tells us again that legendary story of the Queen Mother's visit to Toronto in 1962 when he was the aide-de-camp to Lieut. Gov. John Keiller MacKay.

The Queen Mum was on hand to attend the 103rd running of the Queen's Plate, won that year by Flaming Page, owned by the legendary E.P. Taylor, with famous jockey Jim Fitzsimmons aboard.

Afterward a dinner was held in Her Majesty's honour, with Dick instructed to attend to her needs.

When the first toast comes around, with champagne hoisted, Dick shocks everyone by reaching over and taking her customary gin and tonic out of her hand and replacing it with the champagne.

Her Majesty was not amused. Dick loved to tell that story.

That was the goodbye party for John Slykhuis at Dick Illingworth's house and we all had a great time. Dick is gone now, he lived until age 90 something and was just a great guy. It was one funeral I wanted to attend, but I heard it was going to be chaos with few getting in, so I didn't go. Neither did John, but I always regretted not going.

Years later I was editor of many publications with Citizens Communications Group out of Newmarket and Dick was a prominent freelancer for my business publication – York Business News -- and also my entertainment newspaper – Spotlight.

I'm now 60 years of age and can reflect back on these times and if I can say anything to my readers – enjoy each day because life is fleeting. As my old friend Bruce says, "the only constant in life is change."

POST SCRIPT –As mentioned John Slykhuis is retired and living near Sutton.

I believe artist Dorothy Clark McClure is still with us.

~37~ Alien Attack!

Last Thanksgiving, my good sister Tracy, who you have read about in this book, invited both sides of the clan over for a full turkey dinner. That meant about 16 people. Now Tracy has a big house in Oakville and a large enough dining room that all 16 people could be seated in a square with the centre empty, so it was going to be one big party.

I love going to Tracy's because her husband has a stand-alone beer fridge with all varieties of beer and fully-stocked. After this night, we pretty well emptied it. My wife Aase was into drinking beer that night and so was I, not to mention some of the other guests. Both the Campbell clan and Urquhart clan were on hand.

Now someone on the Urquhart side is prone to panic attacks. We'll call her Nan.

Aase and I arrive at The Campbell's early with all our nightclothes to stay overnight. The house is decorated quite nicely and the smell of turkey and fine foods fills the air. The house seemed quite warm and inviting. Prior to dinner, the brother of Tracy's husband, who has two grown sons that operate a fine film company in Toronto, show off their new flying drone. This thing was a piece of beauty. I think they said it cost $2,500 and can film from the air in HD. Like I said, a thing of beauty.

So we are all in the backyard and they are demonstrating the flying drone, taking our group shot, which was later put on the TV. Tracy's husband gets a brilliant idea – why not take it out front and film the front of the house? If he ever decided to sell his Oakville Ponderosa, it would be a great selling tool. So off they head out the front of the house. They are all standing on the neighbour's lawn right across from the front of the house and the drone is in the air, when all the sudden, Nan shows up with her boyfriend. They are spoiling the filming. They try to park in the driveway, but there are too many cars so they park out front, right in the middle of the drone's filming.

So Tracy's husband starts yelling at them to move further ahead. Nan and her boyfriend can't see the drone, they're totally confused – they don't know what the hell is happening. They both get a look of complete fear on their faces. "Can't we park here? Why not?" What the hell was this – they can't park?

To add to it further, after Nan's boyfriend moves the car ahead and out of the shot, Nan gets out of the car, looking quite distraught and the drone flies right by her head and she screams, "what the hell is that?" with another look of fear on her face. She'd never seen one before.

Tracy's husband settles everybody down and Nan and her boyfriend finally get into the house to start the festivities and dinner, maybe a little bewildered, but they settled down nicely.

POSTSCRIPT – I probably shouldn't have included this chapter, but every time I think of this episode, I laugh my head off.

Surprisingly enough, with all that went on, on her arrival, Nan did not have one of those dreaded panic attacks, which seem to be so prevalent in people with anxiety today.

~38~ Like guns in the Old West

Have you been in a coffee shop, restaurant or movie theatre – or basically any place that people gather – and heard one of those damn cell phones go off? Then you have to sit through a conversation someone else is having?

Have you ever wondered why it is that people have to be accessible by phone 24 hours a day, seven days a week? Have we really gotten that self-important?

Two weeks ago, I took another couple out to a very high-class, upper scale restaurant in Jackson's Point. My male friend, the husband, immediately placed his cell phone on the table as soon as we sat down. You have no idea how this bothered me. (By now, you've probably realized that I don't have any type of mobile phone and will NEVER get one!!!).

Right in the middle of enjoying my lobster and steak dinner, this cell phone goes off. Thank God he retreated outside, despite the cold. But, I thought, you can't even go out for a nice dinner without your cell phone?

Last Friday night I was invited to play some pool at Big Wigs Pool Hall & Bar on Harry Walker Parkway. Again, the first thing my male friend does is lay his cell phone on the table with our drinks. We're joined by another friend, so we're playing two at a time with one sitting out. When it's my friend's turn up, who is sitting down, I look over and he's engaged in an on-line poker game on his cell phone and no-where near ready to resume our 8-Ball game.

Then at my guitar lessons up in Keswick, my teacher says his wife – the mother of a large brood of children and their spouses and now children - goes around prior to a big family dinner and puts these cell phones in a small basket and returns them after the evening is over.

I thought, "what a splendid idea!" Like the Old West, instead of collecting your gun at the door, they now collect cell phones. I really think restaurants, bars, coffee shops and the like, should all do the same thing – collect these damn cell phones!

I was discussing it with my sister who lives in upscale Oakville and she says some high-class restaurants in Oakville are already doing this...Oakville has always been far ahead of the times. This is just such a great idea, I can't fathom why some of Newmarket's, Aurora's and Georgina's finer establishments haven't implemented such a glorious procedure. Save mankind from listening in on some stranger's conversation, whom they could care less about!

After all, the government and lobby groups have been on the backs of smoker's for decades, with the latest eliminating smoking from even bar outside patio areas, thanks to Kathleen Wynne-it-for-all, even though they had already banned these outside patio smoking areas from having roofs or being enclosed in any way. That was thanks to Dalton McSquinty.

But my point is, why are we catering to cell phone users?

Rod Urquhart is an author of humour books, with one published and another on the way.

'Talk Turkey With Urqey' can be purchased at Turn the Page bookstore in Sutton or at Newmarket Public Library.

Rod can be reached at: roderick.urquhart@gmail.com

POST SCRIPT – As printed in The Era, February 22, 2015.

~39~ The final word goes to Big John

FOREWORD – The following is a letter, sent to The Richmond Hill Liberal, when I was Editor in 1984, after I wrote a column on the shameful Leafs. Grammar untouched, as it was originally sent.

Dear Rod:

Rod, Rod, Rod … and (I quote, "murky depths of irrelevance," – "depths of a severe depression???????)" Good God! – if it wasn't for correction fluid (enjoy the fumes, eh?) you may never have captured such a literary smorgasbord of unique and synergistic snappy sayings. But really though, you make me puke with your self-righteous pious condemnation of a fine sporting franchise.

And while on the subject of sports, shall we examine your flaccid figure extensions of Sunday afternoon. Hmmmm?? What excuse say you? You great sodden, tobacco-leached, beer-encrusted wonder. Take heed!

Leave my Leafs alone or all stops shall be pulled on examining your atrib – I won't say attributes, but I don't think that word can be used in a negative or less than zero concept. Ohh well –

How many trees have been felled to support your odorous verbal farts as you wretch your bile-soaked words onto the remains of a once proud organization?

Scum sucker, is this letter reviewed by your publisher? No!!!?? Okay, the things I could tell him!

Having a good day are we? Yes, I'm sure by now, you've looked at all the other papers and your hard-working staff have covered up for your inadequacies and have managed to get yet another rural paper on the stands. Go have a beer. I know how the sound of an operational urinal is music to your ears. And take heart, for most likely this weekend you'll be able to sneak into town and sneak out without further debilitating your already shattered tabletop (hockey)and/or video record with only a dried crust of vomit to mark your passing.

Remember, that in each man's life, the time comes to take the big ride down the sewer, unfortunately yours has no flow.

And in closing, I shall feel a certain sorrow when I pass your door and hear the loud utterings of Aase trying to capture the last malingering life-thread when I know you are yet spending another evening fighting and gallantly, I might add, to keep astray of the depths of a severe depression!

Best regards,

Big John

POSTSCRIPT – As I mentioned earlier, Big John is now retired outside Halifax and we remain very good friends to this day.

~40~ A Blessing you can use

FOREWORD – The following Blessing was given prior to a sit-down meal with our good neighbours, serving them some courses of the Danish Smorgasbord, on December 27, 2014.

Please bow your heads in honour of The Lord and hold the hand of those next to you in friendship.

Welcome to our humble house – the smallest model in Leslie Valley subdivision. But a house is just bricks and mortar. For a house to be a home, it needs smiles, laughter and warmth. Aase and I have this and above all, we are blessed with good friends and family. Not always are the wealthiest men the actual 'richest'. I think a man and his wife blessed with friends and family are really the 'richest of people'. Thank you for being our friends and enjoying some traditional Danish food. We hope you like it!

With all of you here tonight, it makes our house seem much bigger and even warmer!

God Bless everyone here tonight.

Amen

Rod Urquhart

Author Rod Urquhart
at Misener's cottage
around age 18

Rod Urquhart spent 40 years in the newspaper business, mainly in York Region. He's the former Editor of a number of newspaper, magazines and specialty publications, and has appeared on cable television many times.

Rod lives in Newmarket, Ontario with his beloved wife Aase and pooch Heidi.

He's now retired.

He sincerely hopes you've liked his collection of writings and memories.

This is Rod's second book.

If you'd like to reach Rod, simply e-mail:
roderick.urquhart@gmail.com

www.ingramcontent.com/pod-product-compliance
Lightning Source LLC
Chambersburg PA
CBHW061724020426
42331CB00006B/1080